**Margaret Powell** was born in 1907 in Hove, and left school at the age of 13 to start working. At 14, she got a job in a hotel laundry room, and a year later went into service as a kitchen maid, eventually progressing to the position of cook, before marrying a milkman called Albert. In 1968 the first volume of her memoirs, *Below Stairs*, was published to instant success and turned her into a celebrity. She followed this up with *Climbing the Stairs, The Treasure Upstairs* and *The Margaret Powell Cookery Book*. She also co-authored three novels, tie-ins to the television series *Beryl's Lot,* which was based on her life story. She died in 1984.

MARGARET POWELL

# Below Stairs

PAN BOOKS

First published 1968 by Peter Davies Ltd.

First published in paperback 1970 by Pan Books

This edition published 2011 by Pan Books
an imprint of Pan Macmillan, a division of Macmillan Publishers Limited
Pan Macmillan, 20 New Wharf Road, London N1 9RR
Basingstoke and Oxford
Associated companies throughout the world
www.panmacmillan.com

ISBN 978-0-330-53538-0

A CIP catalogue record for this book is available from
the British Library.

Typeset by CPI Typesetting
Printed in the UK by CPI Mackays, Chatham ME5 8TD

Visit **www.panmacmillan.com** to read more about all our books
and to buy them. You will also find features, author interviews
and news of any author events, and you can sign up for e-newsletters
so that you're always first to hear about our new releases.

*To Leigh (Reggie) Crutchley*

*with gratitude and affection*

# Below Stairs

# 1

I WAS BORN in 1907 in Hove, the second child of a family of seven. My earliest recollection is that other children seemed to be better off than we were. But our parents cared so much for us. One particular thing that I always remember was that every Sunday morning my father used to bring us a comic and a bag of sweets. You used to be able to get a comic for a halfpenny plain and a penny coloured. Sometimes now when I look back at it, I wonder how he managed to do it when he was out of work and there was no money at all coming in.

My father was a painter and decorator. Sort of general odd-job man. He could do almost anything: repair roofs, or do a bit of plastering; but painting and paper-hanging were his main work. Yet in the neighbourhood where we lived, there was hardly any work in the winter. People didn't want their houses done up then; they couldn't be painted outside and they didn't want the bother of having it all done up inside. So the winters were the hardest times.

My mother used to go out charring from about eight in the

morning till six in the evening for two shillings a day. Sometimes she used to bring home little treasures: a basin of dripping, half a loaf of bread, a little bit of butter or a bowl of soup. She used to hate accepting anything. She hated charity. But we were so glad of them that, when she came home and we saw that she was carrying something, we used to make a dive to see what she'd got.

It seems funny today, I suppose, that there was this hatred of charity, but when my parents brought us up there was no unemployment money. Anything you got was a charity.

I remember my mother, when we only had one pair of shoes each and they all needed mending, she went down to the council to try to get more for us. She had to answer every question under the sun and she was made to feel that there was something distasteful about her because she hadn't got enough money to live on.

It was very different getting somewhere to live in those days. You just walked through the streets, and there were notices up, 'Rooms to let'.

When we were extra hard up, we only had one room or two rooms in somebody else's house. But when Dad was working, we would go around looking for half a house. We never had a house to ourselves. Not many people could afford a house in those days, not to themselves. As for buying a house, why, such things were never even dreamed of!

I know I used to wonder why, when things were so hard, Mum kept having babies, and I remember how angry she used to get when a couple of elderly spinsters at a house where she worked kept telling her not to have any more children, that she couldn't afford to keep them. I remember saying to my mother, 'Why do you have so many children? Is it hard to have children?' And she said, 'Oh, no. It's as easy as falling off a log.'

You see that was the only pleasure poor people could afford. It cost nothing – at least at the time when you were actually making the children. You could have babies forevermore. Nobody bothered about doctors. You had a midwife who came for almost next to nothing. The fact that it would cost you something later on, well, the working-class people never looked ahead in those days. They didn't dare. It was enough to live for the present.

But, apart from that, people didn't think about regulating families. The whole idea was to have families, a relic of Victorian times perhaps. The more children you had, in some ways, the more you were looked upon as fulfilling your duties as a Christian citizen. Not that the Church played much part in my mother's and father's lives. I don't think they had much time for it or, perhaps it's truer to say, they had time but no inclination. Some of us weren't even christened. I wasn't, and never have been. But we all had to go to Sunday School, not because my parents were religious, but because it kept us out of the way.

Sunday afternoons were devoted to lovemaking because there was not much privacy in working-class families. When you lived in two or three rooms, you had to have some of the children in the same room with you. If you had any sense of decency, and my parents did because I never, during the whole time of my childhood, knew that they ever made love, you waited till they were fast asleep or out of the way. The fact is I never even saw them kissing each other because my father was a rather austere man outwardly, and I was amazed when only lately my mother told me what a passionate man he really was. So, you see, it was only when the children were out of the way that they could really let themselves go.

So, Sunday afternoon, after a mighty big dinner (and everybody tried to have a big dinner on Sunday), was the time spent lying on the bed, making love and having a good old doze. Because, as my Mum said later, if you make love, you might as well do it in comfort. When you're getting middle-aged, there isn't much fun in having it in odd corners. So that's why Sunday School was so popular then. I don't know about now.

My brother and I began proper school together. They let you start at the age of four in those days. My mother sent me there as well because she had another baby coming along and she thought that would be two of us out of the way.

We had to come home for dinner. There were no such things as school meals and school milk. You took a piece of bread and butter with you, wrapped in a piece of paper, and gave it to the teacher to mind, because many of us children were so hungry that we used to nibble it during the course of the morning when we should have been doing whatever we did have to do. It was then doled out to us at eleven o'clock.

My early school days don't stand out much in my mind. It was when I got to the age of about seven that I, as it were, took my place in life. You see, with my mother going off early in the morning to do her charring and me being the eldest girl, I used to have to give the children their breakfast. Mind you, giving them their breakfast wasn't a matter of cooking anything. We never had eggs or bacon, and things like cereals weren't heard of. We had porridge in the winter, and just bread and margarine, and a scraping of jam, if Mum had any, in the summer. Three pieces were all we were allowed.

I always loved going to the baker and buying those round loaves with four corners on top. (I think they were called Coburg loaves.) We used to fight to get the corners because that counted as one piece of bread but it was far more filling than just a slice.

Then I would make the tea, very weak tea known as sweepings – the cheapest that there was – clear away and wash up, and then get ready for school.

The two youngest I took along to the day nursery. It cost sixpence a day each and for that the children got a midday meal as well. I took them just before school time and collected them the moment I came out of school in the afternoon.

At midday, I would run home, get the potatoes and the greens on, lay up the dinner and do everything I could so that when my mother rushed over from work, she just had to serve the dinner.

Generally it was stews because they were the most filling. Sometimes Mother would make a meat pudding. It's funny now when I look back on it, this meat pudding. I would go along to the butcher's and ask for sixpennyworth of 'Block ornaments'. Hygiene was nothing like it is now and butchers used to have big wooden slabs outside the shop with all the meat displayed for the public and the flies. As they cut up the joints, they always had odd lumps of meat left which they scattered around. These were known as 'Block ornaments'.

I used to get sixpennyworth of them and a pennyworth of suet. Then my mother would make the most marvellous meat pudding with it. That tasted far better than those I make now when I pay four or five shillings for the meat.

Directly she'd eaten her dinner, she'd have to rush back to work because she was only allowed half an hour. So I had to do the washing-up before I went back to school again. Right after I came out of school in the afternoon, I would collect the two children from the day nursery, take them back home, and then set to and clear up the place and make the beds.

I never used to feel that I was suffering in any sense from ill-usage. It was just the thing. When you were the eldest girl in a working-class family, it was expected of you.

Of course, Mum took over in the evenings. She came back about six and got us our tea which was the same as breakfast – bread and margarine.

Being a girl, I never went out at night and my parents were very strict about this. But I used to read a lot. We had a free library even then. We also managed to amuse ourselves.

My oldest brother used to give magic shows. He was really very good. Then somebody gave us a magic lantern with slides, of course not moving, and my brother would make up a story about them. We were never bored with an evening. There was always something to do.

Unlike so many people I've met, I didn't really make any lasting friends in my school days. I suppose it's easy to look back and say my mother and father weren't sociable because we weren't allowed to have friends in. Mum had enough children of her own. I never had birthday parties, of course; things like that were undreamt of.

I had two girls at school who were friends but you know what it's like when you're three together, someone is the odd one out and that was always me. I think these two girls came from homes where things were talked about, things like sex, because they used to have a sort of code between them which would make them screech with mirth, and I never understood a word. I remember when I was nearly thirteen years old, one of them, her name was Bertha, wouldn't run around and play with us. And I asked 'Why? Why can't you run about?' 'Oh,' she said, 'I had a bicycle out yesterday and it hurt me, and I can't do anything now.' And they both went off into screams of mirth.

But, being a member of a family, I wasn't worried and, you see, we had the town itself.

# 2

HOVE WAS a wonderful place, especially for children, and particularly for children with no money. It wasn't built up as it is now.

Take the seafront and the lawns. Each lawn is laid out for people with money now. There are clock golf, putting, tennis, bowls; but there's nowhere for children at all. But then, every one of those lawns was free; there was nothing on them but grass and a shelter, and all around the lawns there were shrubs where you could have the most marvellous games of hide-and-seek. You could take your tea down there, spread it all over the clean grass. There were no park keepers to come and chivvy you.

And immediately behind the town was the country. We only had to walk a matter of minutes from where we lived and there was the country and the farms.

The farmers were so friendly to you; they let you walk around; hang over the pigsty, scratch the pigs, cluck at the chickens and watch them milking the cows. Often the farmer's wife would come out with a glass of lemonade for us.

There were trees to climb, marvellous trees which seemed to have grown just for children.

Back on the beach, there were the seaside shows, the Pierrot shows. It was sixpence or a shilling to sit down in a deckchair and watch it, but, needless to say, we never had money like that. So we used to stand at the back.

Looking back, I think the shows were good. Not in the least smutty because it was meant as a family show.

A soprano would come on and sing a soulful song about lost love, how she once had a lover and the lover had departed through some misunderstanding and she hoped with all her heart they would come together again. Half the audience were in tears, and so were we kids at the back. People believed in things like that then; dying for love, feeling soulful about it, regret, lost opportunities and all that kind of thing. None of this 'couldn't care less' attitude. Then there was the baritone. He would sing songs about friendship, England, and 'Hands Across the Sea'.

All this would be considered very small beer nowadays but we thought it was wonderful and so did the audience.

Then there were the donkeys, and the donkey man who looked after them. Now I've heard it said that people who have much to do with animals get like them both in appearance and mannerisms. So the donkey man resembled his charges. He was old, small, bowed down, grey, and very hairy. He didn't exactly have a beard. Hair seemed to be sprouting out all over him. I thought to myself many a time, if he got down on all fours you could have got on his back and you wouldn't have known you were not on a donkey.

What a poor sorry lot those donkeys were! I suppose they had enough to eat, but donkeys always look such pathetic creatures unless they are well looked after, and these presumably weren't. But the well-to-do children never had to sit on the back of a donkey like the common children. Certainly not! They might get polluted. They sat in a little dogcart, all done up in red leather. It held two. These children with nannies to look after them used to come down in style in large prams.

Not only did the man who owned the dogcart have to walk along the one side, but the nanny had to walk along the other. Because no harm must come to those darlings. Though it didn't matter about us jogging along on the back of the old donkeys getting saddle sores.

Wealthy children were never allowed to play with low-class children like us. They were never allowed to play with anyone but similarly wealthy children. They never went anywhere on their own without their nannies. Some of them had two, a nurse and an under-nurse. The lawns were open to everybody, and they couldn't keep us away from them, but if any child wandered up to us, its nurse would say, 'Come away! Come away this instant! Come over here.' They'd never let them speak to us.

Mind you, we had a kind of contempt for them. They couldn't do the things that we could do. They weren't allowed to dirty their clothes like we were. They weren't allowed to run in and out of the bushes. They weren't allowed to climb all over the seats and walk along the very narrow tops of them. They weren't allowed to do anything exciting. It wasn't their fault.

So we never mixed, never. They played their dainty little games with large coloured balls. They pushed their dolls' prams around and rode on their scooters.

We had nothing except perhaps an old tennis ball, but still we used to have the most marvellous games with absolutely nothing at all.

Perhaps if we had been allowed to mix, we would have become quite friendly but I don't think so because they were brought up with an ingrained idea that they were a different class of people from us altogether.

For instance, I remember one occasion when I was playing on the lawns, I had a coat on which had originally been my grandmother's. It was a plush affair. One of these children came over and started making remarks about my coat. The nanny said to her, 'Oh, you shouldn't say things like that, dear, after all they're poor children. Their mummy hasn't got any money.' And the child said, 'Haw, haw, but doesn't she look funny? I wonder if Mummy has got anything she could give her to wear.' I was simply furious because I hadn't minded the coat. I hadn't felt that because it was my grandmother's coat there was something wrong about wearing it. But although this incident has stuck in my mind I soon got over my feelings of resentment because there was always something to do or something to look forward to, like the yearly visit to the circus.

# 3

THE BEST circus we ever had was Lord George Sanger's. I suppose his name was George Lord and he turned it around, but we used to think he was a real lord. He dressed up so well we thought he was marvellous, in a leather jacket with fringes hanging all around, a huge Stetson hat and a sort of riding trousers, with shiny boots that came up to his knees in a point with metal studs up the side. We thought that was how a lord should dress. It was something out of this world. We couldn't always afford to go to his circus, but we would do our utmost. Still, you could always walk around and look at all the animals – the elephants, the lions, and tigers. That was all free.

One particular year they came down, I remember, and billed as a marvellous attraction was a man who was shot from a cannon, right across the tent, and landed in a net. Every night we could hear the tremendous 'Boom!' as the cannon went off. This made our longing to go even stronger but it was during one of my father's out-of-work periods. He just couldn't give us the money. It was sixpence each for children to go in. That is for sitting right at the back. So we set about getting the money. We went along the streets knocking on people's doors asking for old jam jars they didn't want. We didn't have any jam jars in our house. When we bought jam it was by the pennyworth in a cup, doled out from seven-pound jars. The grocer was a friend of mine, and used to make a fuss of me. After he'd doled out my penny-worth of jam in a great big wooden spoon, he always used to give me the spoon to lick. It was marvellous.

So we got all the jam jars we could and took them to the rag-and-bone shop. You had to get six, I think, for a penny. Then we went out getting manure. Threepence a barrow we got for it. It was easy because there used to be the corporation cart horses. Every day the cart came around with a sprinkler on the back and watered the roads. When it got to our house, it was the end of the round. The driver used to go into a nearby café and leave his two horses outside. Whether it was because it was the end of the round or whether they were tired, they always used to oblige by dropping a large load of manure. Before the man went into the café, he used to put nosebags on the horses to feed them and tremendous flocks of pigeons would come around to pick up the bits that fell from the bags. We used to run under the horses' legs to shovel up the manure, and the pigeons would fly into the air startling the horses. How we never got kicked to death I don't know.

Then sometimes we would follow a pantechnicon through the street waiting for it to stop and the horses to oblige. So it didn't take very long to fill a barrow with a load of manure.

When I look back on it, we must have been very honest. We didn't just pile it up. We would pat it all down with our shovels so that people really did have their money's worth. It used to surprise us that, with so much of the stuff lying around, people were willing to pay for it.

After several days of this selling of jam jars and collecting manure, we managed to accumulate half a crown which, at sixpence each, was the entrance money for the five of us.

So the great day came. It was like a fairy tale. A girl dressed in glittering tights came on leading four or five elephants. She let the elephants pick her up in their trunks. Then she would lie on the floor and let them step over her.

The lions came on and roared suitably. As part of the act a man put his head right into the lion's mouth. I couldn't watch.

Another thing I couldn't watch was the aerial trapeze.

But the high spot of the evening for us was the man to he shot from the cannon. The night before we went, we'd heard Mum saying to Dad that when this act had been on in America, the man didn't land in the net the right way and he broke his neck. Well, with the callousness of children, we didn't think it was a bad thing at all. Suppose it happened when we went. After all, he had been doing it for several nights and it was time he had a mishap.

It was the very last act of all. We saw him climb in feet first. Then came the 'Boom' we'd anticipated. Out he shot in a cloud of smoke. I must admit I didn't see him sail to the other side of the tent. I suppose he must have done. He landed in the net quite safely, and there was a tremendous burst of applause which we joined in. Mind you, we would have given just as much applause if he had broken his neck.

It was a marvellous evening. I didn't go to sleep that night thinking about it all.

# 4

ANOTHER DIVERSION which may seem a commonplace now was the cinema but, of course, it bore no comparison with films today. The places by present standards were sleazy.

The one we liked was in the main street. The films were livelier and so were the serials. It used to be on every evening and Saturday afternoon. In the evenings the prices were sixpence, ninepence, a shilling, and one and threepence, but on Saturday afternoon children could get in for three halfpence if you sat downstairs, or threepence if you sat in the gallery. All the well-to-do children, well-to-do by our standards that is, went upstairs and subjected us to an avalanche of orange peelings and nutshells.

Infants in arms went in for nothing. We used to stagger up to the box office with three- and four-year-olds in our arms so that we didn't have to pay for them. The moment we passed the box office, we put them down and let them walk.

We would all go into the cinema at least an hour before the film began. During that hour, a tremendous uproar would go on. There was a woman who always played the piano. Her name was Miss Bottle or so we always called her. She was a middle-aged spinster who had her hair scraped back in a bun with what appeared to be a hatpin skewered through it at the back. She had the most tremendous bosom. Women didn't wear falsies in those days so I suppose it was natural. About a quarter of an hour before she was due to arrive, we used to stamp our feet on the floor and cry out, 'Miss Bottle! Miss Bottle!' She must have been flattered, and when she did appear, Paderewski could not have received a greater ovation than Miss Bottle did. Not that we cared the least about the music or the fact that she played the piano, it was because when she appeared we knew that the film was just going to start.

During the whole time that we were in the cinema, there was nothing but pandemonium. Babies were howling and the kids were screeching. But it didn't matter because they were silent films. We did all the talking that there was.

Just before the film began, the manager used to come on stage with a megaphone and bawl through it, 'Quiet! Quiet!' Then, oozing benevolence, his face wreathed in smiles, he used to say, 'Now, kiddies, you are going to have a marvellous time this afternoon. You're going to see two lovely films, and I know you are going to enjoy yourselves so when you go home, don't forget to tell your mummies and daddies what a good time you've had.' Then his face would change. The smile would be wiped off, and glaring at us ferociously, he would say, 'Look after the babies and don't you let the little buggers wet the seats!' But we never used to care. We used to stamp our feet and scream. Nobody took a bit of notice of him.

Then began the main film and Miss Bottle played all the way through. When I think of the stamina of those pianists! When the action was fierce, she would bang on the keys and put her foot down on the pedal to get it as loud as possible. In the romantic love scenes, she would play soft melodious tunes and the kids used to put their fingers in their mouths and whistle. We didn't care tuppence about love in those days.

The serial was often the most harrowing thing. It also used to be our bugbear because there were some weeks when we couldn't afford to go. Dad would be out of work and he couldn't even give us the three halfpennies we needed to get in. It always happened when the serial had reached a most thrilling episode like the heroine being suspended over a cliff or tied on the railway line or fixed just in front of a circular saw coming nearer and nearer to her. Then up would come the words, 'To be continued next week'. The times I've hung around the cinema that next week waiting for my friends to come out to tell me what had happened. It never occurred to me that she wouldn't really get killed, that she couldn't because the serial had to go on. I used to ask, 'What happened to her? Did she get killed? How did she get away?' So really the serials were a terrible worry to me.

# 5

THE SHOPS, of course, were nothing like the shops there are now. There were no such things as supermarkets or self-service stores. They were mostly little family concerns.

There was a Woolworth's. I don't think it was called Woolworth's in those days. It was the 'Thruppenny and Sixpenny Bazaar'. Everything in it was either threepence or sixpence. You would have thought that at these prices there couldn't have been much variety but the way they used to get over it was most ingenious. They would separate things. For instance, sixpence for a kettle and threepence for the lid, not sold separately so, you see, it was still sixpence and threepence. The same with saucepans, cups and saucers and so on. Nevertheless, for sixpence, you could get a great many things.

The pawnshop played a big part in working-class people's lives. Every Monday morning the wives would cart their husbands' suits along to put them in pawn and have enough money to get them through the week. On Friday night or Saturday morning, they'd be along to get them out so that the husbands could wear them on Saturdays and Sundays. On Monday, back they would go again. In very hard times, other things would go in, like sheets and blankets. You didn't get a lot of money on them but even a shilling or two helped you through the week.

Then, of course, the little grocers' shops were a great standby. They were always ready to give tick. Mother would send me along with a note saying could she have this, that, and the other on her list and she would pay at the end of the week. They would let you do it because people always paid when they could. Mostly everybody was poor and relied on getting things on tick. The shops may not have been as attractive as they are today but I'm sure the food had more flavour.

Take the baker's shop on the corner of our road. It was the most wonderful shop to us! You see they really baked the bread there, and the glorious smell greeted us on our way to school in the morning. Even if you weren't hungry the wonderful smell of that bread would make your mouth water. They used to do doughnuts for a halfpenny each. Not the sort of doughnuts that you find now that are a lump of dough. One bite and you haven't found the jam; another and you've passed it. They were gorgeous, greasy, and golden, coated in fine sugar, and loaded with jam. The baker used to make several batches a day. On a weekend when Dad got his money, for a treat we would have some of these for tea. They beat any cakes that I've ever known now. And so did the bread. It wasn't like this kind of bread you eat now that tastes like cotton-wool in your mouth, you can chew it for ever and it's like swallowing lumps of wet dough. It was like cake. Of course by present-day standards, it wasn't hygienic. None of it was wrapped.

When I was a girl practically every street had a pub, in fact some streets had one on each corner.

Saturday night was the main drinking night. The gaiety there had to be seen to be believed. I can well understand why. You see, employers in those days were vastly different from what they are now. Today 'Jack's as good as his master', but in those days he certainly wasn't. It was 'Yes, sir', 'No, sir' and work from morning till night. And work hard because if you didn't there were half a dozen people queuing up to take your place. But when you got in the pub you were your own master. Yes, then a man had money in his pocket regardless of the fact that it was supposed to last him all the week. So he let go. He went in the pub and aired his opinions and there was no boss to dictate to him. He could say what he liked. Mostly the men got over there as soon as the pub opened and the women as soon as they put the kids to bed. Many women took their children with them – leaving them outside the doors.

On a Saturday night, by eight o'clock, it would be absolute bedlam inside. There'd be all the people singing and dancing. There was always music. Somebody would play a concertina; somebody a banjo. Somebody would give a turn singing. The men would be swearing at the top of their voices, and often the women as well.

And the kids outside. Some of them would be in prams; some would be playing; some would open the door and bawl,

'Mum, aren't you coming out? Mum, baby's howling!' And out would come mother. She'd either give the baby something or she'd cuff all her offspring for getting her out and back she would dart in again. Of course, when it came to closing time there was nearly always a free fight on the pavement. They just fought with their fists and shouted obscenities. There was no knocking them down and kicking them in the balls or using knives and bottles like you get now.

There used to be one man whose wife didn't drink. When he came out of the pub, three sheets in the wind, reeling along, he'd look up at his bedroom window. If he saw a light on, he knew she'd gone to bed and he'd bawl out, 'It's no good you bloody well going to sleep, you old cow, because I shall need you in a minute!'

There was nothing else for working-class people but the pubs. They couldn't afford to go to the theatres; the cinema maybe. It wasn't that they spent such a lot. The beer was so strong then. When my Dad was in work he used to come home Saturday at dinnertime and send me around to the bottle-and-jug department to get half a pint of Burton. They used to have only this half a pint between them. But my mother said it was just like drinking wine, it was so strong and smooth that that was as much as they needed. Nowadays you can down pints of the stuff and all it does is fill you full of wind and water.

# 6

ALTHOUGH WE lived by the sea a lot of our playing was done in the streets. It is nowadays to some extent, but then we used to play proper games. The games were marvellous because not only did you have the pavement, you had the road as well. There wasn't much traffic then.

At Easter, for example, it was street skipping. We'd get a long scaffold rope out, stretching from one side of the street to the other. The mothers would turn the rope and anyone who liked could skip in. Sometimes there would be a dozen all skipping at the same time and singing, 'Hot cross buns, one a penny, two a penny, hot cross buns.'

Another game was Buttons. How my mother used to dread the autumn when Button time came around! We used to draw a chalk square on the pavement by the house and shoot the buttons into it. The first person who managed to get her button into the square and knock somebody else's out won them all. I was an absolute duffer at the game.

Then there was hopscotch time. You drew a big oblong in

chalk on the pavement and squared it off, and numbered these squares from one up to twelve. Then you threw a stone first into 'One', then you hopped into that square, picked up the stone and bopped the way around without touching the lines. Next you threw the stone into 'Two' and hopped and picked up the stone in 'Two' and hopped all the way around again, and so on till you'd put the stone in all the squares. The moment you put the other foot down or you didn't succeed in picking up the stone, you were out.

Marbles was the game everybody went mad about. You kicked a hole in the road about six or seven feet from the gutter. And you could then. The idea was to get the marbles into the hole – and the game developed in the same way as Buttons. Yet another game was hoops. My aunt bought me the largest hoop you could have. It had an iron guide which you hooked on to the hoop and I ran all round the roads with it. You never had to worry about traffic. No child would last very long doing that today.

Then, of course, there was top time. That was a wonderful time because these tops you just wound up with string and you could whip them from one end of the street to the other. You could paste little coloured pieces of paper on the top of them so that when you whipped, it was like a rainbow going round.

Later in the autumn, we used to go up to the Downs and get horse-chestnuts and play conkers. It didn't cost us anything. And as soon as we lost one supply we could always get more.

I don't want to give the impression that life was all games.

There was always school and the holidays weren't as long as they are now, but I always enjoyed going to school because I did pretty well there. I never found any of it hard except things like art, knitting, and needlework. None of those things were any good to me at all. The needlework was my biggest hate. We had to make such ugly garments; chemises and bloomers – as they were called then. Both made of calico. The chemises were wide with sort of cap sleeves and they reached down to the knees. The bloomers did up at the back with buttons and were also voluminous. Whoever bought these awful garments when they were finished I really don't know. I should imagine they were given to the workhouse because I certainly never brought any home. There were always loads of gathers and you had to stroke the gathers. I was absolutely hopeless at it. In the first place, I could never seem to get on with the thimble. So, of course, I used to prick my finger and the garments got spotted with blobs of blood. It started out as a white garment but it was red and black by the time I'd finished. Well, can you wonder at it? There were the most primitive lavatories in the yard but there was nowhere to wash your hands. So I came in after playtime with my hands filthy to do this needlework.

Singing was hopeless too. I always remember the school concert. We had a concert once a year and, as I was always a bit of a big head, I thought that I would be able to do something. The teacher said to me, 'You can't sing.' So she said, 'I know what you can do. You can tell a funny story. I'll write it all out for you and you learn it all off by heart.'

The funny story was about a man who went into a café

and wanted a plate of boiled onions. He got so muddled with it that he asked for a plate of oiled bunions. I thought it was quite funny. So did my family. They got the joke presumably. But when it came to the concert and I got up on the platform I started saying it in a very straight way – sort of parrot fashion, and then I got my onions and bunions all the wrong way round and at the end I waited for the laugh but nobody did except the teachers. They had to laugh. It was terrible. I never felt so mortified in my life. I went as red as a beetroot, and left in a great hurry. They never got me to do anything else. They had no manners at all. They should have laughed. Especially as it was free.

But the great thing about school in those days was that we had to learn. I don't think you can beat learning; how to read and write, and how to do arithmetic. Those are the three things that anyone who has got to work for a living needs. We were forced to learn and I think children need to be forced. I don't believe in this business of 'if they don't want to do it, it won't do them any good'. It *will* do them good. Our teacher used to come around and give us a mighty clump on the neck or box on the ears if she saw us wasting our time. Believe me, by the time we came out of school, we came out with something. We knew enough to get us through life. Not that any of us thought about what we were going to do. We all knew that when we left school we'd have to do something, but I don't think we had any ambitions to do any particular type of work.

# 7

I WON A SCHOLARSHIP when I was thirteen which was the age one sat for it then. You had to say on your paper what you would like to be. I said I wanted to be a teacher. My parents saw my headmistress but when they found out that I couldn't possibly earn any money till I was eighteen and up to that time they would have to keep me, and not only keep me, but buy my books and clothes, they just couldn't do it. You see, there were no government grants in those days.

I was allowed to leave school because I was in the top class and if I had put in another year it would have been the same work all over again.

Looking back, I wish it had been possible to have gone on with my education but at that time I didn't mind in the least. I didn't think my parents were hard because I knew I had to go out to work, I knew we needed the money so desperately. I had known the mortifications of poverty. I remember when I was about seven – it was early in the Great War. Dad wasn't called up then but nobody was having anything done in the

27

decorating line; the men had gone into the army and money was very tight indeed.

That was when the town opened the soup kitchen. It was in Sheridan Terrace, Hove. A covered stone building with two coal-burning coppers. You queued up for your helping at midday – that was the only time they served it. The soup was terrible. Thin, watery pea soup. I'm sure it was the kind of stuff they doled out to Oliver Twist. I had to go up there with a washstand jug to get it. Mum never knew what shame that washstand jug caused me. It was a white one covered in pink roses. Other children had enamel jugs which seemed to me a far more suitable thing. And to walk through the streets, carrying a large washstand jug full of pea soup pretending you hadn't been up there and got it for nothing, that you've not been accepting charity, well, then you've got to be very clever indeed. I wouldn't let Mother know how it made me feel because there was no one else to do it.

When my father got called up in 1916 the separation allowance was terrible. It really was. Starvation money. That's all you could call it.

Then the coal got in short supply. You couldn't have even half a hundredweight of coal if you had a gas stove. So I used to have to go down to the Town Hall, young as I was, to get a permit. I swore 'black's blue' that we hadn't got a gas stove, that we'd never had a gas stove, that we did all our cooking on the fire, and I never turned a hair. Can you wonder that you grow up with all your wits around you? Then when I'd got this permit, I had to go right up to the depot where the trains came in and wait there in a queue. It was winter, it was freezing cold and my stomach was empty. I pushed the coal back in an old pram and I fainted with the cold. Somebody picked me up and took me into their house. They gave me something to eat and a sixpence but I still had to push the coal back home.

With my father gone, it was a harrowing time. I remember Mother used to confide in me, the eldest girl. I remember when we hadn't anything left to use for warmth and no money to get coal. I said to Mum, 'Get all the wood down. Let's have a fire with wood.' She took every single shelf there was in the rooms and she even took the banisters from the stairs. Things like this make you hard.

I had also adopted a kind of grown-up manner with all the shops. The butcher in particular, he was a great favourite of mine. I used to go along there on a weekend and say, 'I want the biggest joint you've got for a shilling.' He used to say, 'Well, I hope you've brought your own paper.' So I would say, 'Oh, yes, I have. I've brought this bus ticket to wrap it in. That's large enough for your joints.'

Every other morning, Mum got my brother and me up at six o'clock. She gave us sixpence and a pillowcase and we went to the baker's — Forfar's in Church Road. They didn't open till eight o'clock but the earlier you got there, the better bread you got. It took us about twenty minutes to walk it so we had a long wait outside.

If we were first in the queue, we used to look through the letterbox and see just what sort of bread they had. Mostly it was large flat brown loaves. We used to call them cow cakes

29

because they resembled the cow-dung that we saw in the fields. Especially when people had trodden on it.

Sometimes we'd see a currant loaf. It was marvellous if we got a currant loaf.

For our sixpence they used almost to fill a pillowcase with bread.

Best of all were the rolls. If there were any rolls put in, we used to eat them on the way home and never say a word to Mum. We were so ravenous, getting up at six, queuing outside in all that cold, so just eating those odd rolls was absolute heaven.

The best thing that happened around our street during the war was when they billeted the soldiers on us.

My mother had three. An Englishman, a Scotsman, and an Irishman. She had to ask to have the Irishman removed. He made such uproars and all that.

I don't know what the money was, but I noticed there was a change in our standard of living. Mum said my father wasn't too keen about the idea. You see she was an attractive woman and he was in France at the time and couldn't do anything about it.

It made a big difference. All of a sudden everybody sprouted out with new things. Even the tally-man got paid. The tally-man was a door-to-door salesman. He came around and sold sheets and pillowcases, and boots and shoes, and things like that, carrying them in a large case. You paid him so much a week for the goods and a little bit over the odds because he had to wait for his money. You never signed agreements, it was just written down in a book. Selling the goods was easy. Anyone could buy them but when it came to collecting the money it was a different story indeed. When Mother had no money I used to stand at the top of the steps watching for the tally-man. When I saw him coming I used to rush in and bawl out, 'He's here, Mum!' and she used to go and hide. When he came to the door I would answer and say, 'Mum's out.' He never used to believe me and he used to get very abusive, but of course he couldn't do anything. The same with the rent collector. There just wasn't the money.

I would have nightmares about this rent collector and the fact that he might turn us out. Everything got paid eventually but that was the trouble, you see, running up debts so that when your husband got work again, you were still as hard up in a way because you were paying off what had accumulated while he was out of work.

# 8

I STARTED WORK the first week after I left school. It was a housework job in a bungalow, with a married couple. The wife was an old lady, a semi-invalid, paralysed from the waist down. I worked from seven in the morning until one, Sundays included, for ten shillings a week. I didn't get any dinner because that was the idea of leaving at one o'clock just as they were starting their dinner, but I did get breakfast.

The funny part about this breakfast, although I didn't think so then, was that it was anything that was left from the night before. Sometimes I had milk pudding, sometimes I had macaroni cheese, sometimes I had cottage pie. But I didn't worry. I ate everything there was because the more I ate down there the less my Mum had to give me. Food was getting to be a constant problem with me because although I was only thirteen, I was a huge girl and I had an enormous appetite. And of course the harder I worked, the hungrier I got. My mother used to get so indignant about this breakfast. She said it was such a cheat giving me things like that.

I should have eggs and bacon, and not the old left-overs. But I never used to worry, I couldn't care less what I ate so long as I did.

I didn't stay at that job very long mainly because I began to develop pains in my legs. I presume it was because I was beginning to mature. I remember one morning I had such pains in my legs, I said to the man of the house, 'I can't work any more today. My legs hurt me so much.' He gave me a bottle of liniment to rub them with and said it would do them extra good because it was horse liniment. I was furious. I could hardly walk. So that finished that job.

That first year I had a dozen jobs altogether. These little daily jobs were all the same. I was very young so they paid me a microscopic wage, but at the same time I looked so hefty that they expected a lot out of me.

One job which I had lasted only a week. It was to push a cantankerous old lady around in a bathchair. She had once been somebody by the aristocratic way in which she spoke, but she was reduced to one old retainer to look after her and a large-sized house.

Every morning it was my job to go there and help this old lady into her bathchair. And that was a business, believe me, what with the bonnets, the capes, and the button boots. All the time I was doing this for her she was nagging at me. When I got her ensconced in this bathchair I had to push her round to the shops, and then go and say, 'Mrs Graham is outside. Will you please come out for orders?' Can you imagine nowadays going into a shop and asking the shopkeeper to come out for orders? But in those days, although she was as poor as a church mouse, with her aristocratic manner, the shop keepers would come out, very obsequiously bow and scrape and later send everything that she ordered.

Nothing I did was right for her. Either I hadn't got her into the right position outside the shop or the sun was in her eyes or I'd jolted her back.

One particular day, it was a lovely summer morning and she wanted me to push her along the seafront. We went down to the West Pier, about a mile and a half. Then she wanted me to arrange her chair so that the wind was at the back of her and yet so she could still see the people. She was at her worst that day, and she moaned the whole journey, so that after I tried to get her into position about six times and still it wasn't right, I just gave up. I didn't say anything. I just walked away and left her. I never did know what happened to her or how she got back or anything.

When I told Mother she was taken aback at first, but when she told Dad he saw the funny side of it and all through the week he kept saying, 'I wonder if that old girl is still stuck at the West Pier?'

After that, as a change from housework, I got a job in a sweet shop. Every child's delight. I was allowed to eat as many sweets as I wanted. I was soon sick of them. The reason I got the sack from there was that all my brothers and sisters and their friends used to come in with their halfpennies and farthings. I used to dole them out sweets *ad lib* and the owner saw all her profit going.

The job I was really waiting for was to work at the local laundry, but you had to be fourteen before they would start you there. I went at thirteen and a half, thinking that, as I was such a big person, they would take me on, but they asked to see my birth certificate so that was that.

As soon as I was fourteen I went there and got taken on as a sorter. I was put in a room on my own and had to sort the linen from the Hotel Metropole, the biggest hotel in Brighton. That was my job for the first six months. Afterwards I got to running around for everybody, a bit in the ironing room and a bit in the washroom.

I worked from eight o'clock until six for twelve and six-pence a week. Not a lot of money and no meals. But it was lively, far livelier than doing housework, especially the iron-ing room. The language and the atmosphere there reminded me of Dante's *Inferno*.

It was one of my jobs to go into this room with a watering-can to sprinkle the floor, because there were no mechanical means of removing the dust and with the clothes being continually moved around the floor used to get covered with a fine white powder. If by chance you sprinkled the water on the feet of the ironing women instead of on the floor, they used to swear like Billingsgate fishwives. I'd never heard anything like it in my life, even on a Saturday night along our street, and they used to tell the foulest jokes and screech with mirth at my incomprehension.

What a sight I must have looked. It was the time when girls were wearing boots that came up to the knees but I had a pair that came just above my ankles like my father's boots. I was already taking size eights although I was only fourteen. In the morning I never knew whether they were Dad's or mine until

I had examined them well. So what with that and the jumper my mother had knitted me (she had run out of the wool when she got to the back so it was a different colour from the front) and my hair straight back, and the goitre from which I was suffering, I must have looked like a drawing by Boz.

When I got to be fifteen and was due for a half a crown rise, I got the sack. They had no need to pay you fifteen shillings a week. Girls of fourteen could do what I was doing. So that any excuse they found to get rid of you, they did.

# 9

WHEN I CAME home from the laundry and told my mother I'd got the sack she was very annoyed. I expect she was a bit fed up, with all the various jobs I'd had since I left school, and she said, 'I did think you were settled at the laundry. You were mad keen to go there at fourteen, and now you've got the sack at fifteen. Oh well, there's nothing else for it, you'll have to go into domestic service, that's all.'

I hated the idea but I never even thought of moaning about it. I dare say I could have appealed to my father because he always made a big fuss of me; although Mum was the guiding light in our house – Dad left everything to her. We've always done as my mother told us to do. Children did at that time.

So I said, 'All right, then.' I didn't know that much about it – and my mother told me what a good job it was; all the benefits that accrue from going into service; good food and lodgings and that. The money you do get is all your own.

Of course, like a lot of things seen in retrospect, my mother looked at her years in domestic service through a vista of married life, with a husband always out of work in the winter, with seven children and never enough money for food, never mind about clothes. Her years in domestic service seemed a time when at least she did have a certain amount of money that she could call her own.

She forgot the tales she used to tell us – how she went into it when she was fourteen years old in 1895, and how she had to work like a galley slave; an object of derision to the other servants.

So when I reminded Mum of all this, 'Ah,' she said, 'life is different in service now; the work's not so hard, you get more free time, and the outings and money are better.'

So I said, 'Well, what could I be in service, then?' and she said, 'Well, as you hate needlework' (and I always did hate needlework) 'there's only one place you can go and that is into the kitchen. If you're a parlourmaid you've got to mend all the table linen, and if you're a housemaid you've got to mend all the house linen, and if you're in the nursery you've got to mend, and even make, the children's clothes. But if you're a kitchen maid, then you don't have any needlework to do at all.' So I said, 'All right, then, I'll be a kitchen maid.'

I went down to a domestic agency, of which there were a great many at that time; and many posts for kitchen maids, because it was the lowest position in the house for a servant. Yet it's funny, you know, if you wanted to be a cook and you had no money to pay for training, the only way you could learn to be one was by starting as a kitchen maid.

I was offered various posts and eventually I settled on one

in Adelaide Crescent in Hove, because it was fairly near to where we lived. It was the home of the Reverend Clydesdale and his wife. My mother came with me for the interview.

They were tremendous houses in Adelaide Crescent; they started off with a basement and went right up to an attic, there were a hundred and thirty-two stairs in all, and the basements were dark and like dungeons. The front of the basement, with iron bars all down the bay windows, was the servants' hall. When you were sitting in there all you saw going by was people's legs, and when you were on the other side of the basement hall, which was the kitchen, a big conservatory overhung that, so you saw nothing at all. It had one tiny window high up in the wall which you couldn't see through unless you got a ladder. The light had to be on all day long.

The Crescent is one of the most imposing in Hove. The houses were Regency style, and even now, although they are all flats, they haven't altered the façade, and it still looks very much as it did with gardens right down the centre. Of course, at that time only the residents had keys and were allowed to use the gardens, but that certainly didn't apply to the servants, I can assure you.

When my mother and I arrived at this house for the interview we went to the front door. In all the time I worked there, that was the only time I ever went in by the front door. But the front door it was on this particular day. We were ushered into a hall that I thought was the last word in opulence. There was a lovely carpet on the floor, and tremendously wide stairs carpeted right across, not like the tiny little bit of lino in the middle we had on our stairs. There was a great mahogany table in the hall and a mahogany hallstand, and huge mirrors with gilt frames. The whole thing breathed an aura of wealth to me. I thought they must be millionaires. I'd never seen anything like it.

A butler opened the door to us and my mother said that this was Margaret Langley who had come for the interview as a kitchen maid. A very tiny little butler he was. I'd always thought that butlers were tall, imposing men. In the hall we saw a rather elderly gentleman and the lady who was to interview us. We were shown into what was obviously a nursery – a day nursery.

My mother did all the talking because I was overcome with wonder at this room, for although it was only a nursery, you could have put all the three rooms that we lived in into it. Also I was overcome with shyness; I suffered agonies of self-consciousness in those days. And the lady, Mrs Clydesdale, looked me up and down as though I was something at one of those markets, you know, one of those slave markets. She seemed to be weighing up all my points.

My mother told her that I had been doing daily jobs. She didn't mention the laundry because she didn't think that was any recommendation. People thought that laundries were hotbeds of vice in those days because of the obscene language of the girls who worked there.

Mrs Clydesdale decided that because I was strong and healthy I would do. I was to have twenty-four pounds a year, paid monthly. I was to have one afternoon and evening off from four o'clock to ten o'clock, and alternate Sundays off the same hours, and I was never to be in later than ten o'clock under any circumstances. I was to have three print dresses, blue or green; four white aprons with bibs, and four caps; stockings, and black strapped shoes. I was always to say 'Sir' and 'Madam' if I was spoken to by Mr and Mrs Clydesdale, and I was to treat the upper servants with great respect and do everything the cook asked me to do. To all these things my mother said, 'Yes, Madam, no, Madam', and all these things she promised on my behalf that I would do. My spirits sank lower and lower. I felt I was in jail at the finish.

When we got outside I told Mum how I felt but she'd decided that the job would do for me. So that was that.

The trouble was the uniform. My mother worked it out that it couldn't be done – all these things that had to be bought for me – under two pounds. I know that it sounds a ridiculously small sum now, but two pounds was untold wealth to us then. We hadn't got two pounds but anyway she managed to borrow it and she fitted me out.

On the day I was due to go there she got her old, battered tin trunk that she'd been all through domestic service with, and I packed the few things that I had in it. Apart from the uniform my own clothes were very few indeed. I was dressed up in a blouse and skirt and a coat that had belonged to my grandmother.

I said to Mum, 'How are we going to get the tin trunk down to Adelaide Crescent? Are we going to have a taxi?' She said, 'You must be stark, raving mad. Where do you think we are going to get the money from? Dad's going to borrow the barrow.' Dad worked for a decorator at that time, so he was going to load the trunk on to the barrow and wheel it down there. We must have looked a peculiar lot – my Dad walking in the road with the tin trunk on the barrow, and Mum and I trailing along on the pavement. When we got there Dad carried the tin trunk down to the basement.

As she said goodbye my Mum put her arms around me, which was very unusual because in our family we didn't indulge in any outward show of affection. I felt as if I could have howled and howled. And yet they weren't going miles away, they lived in the same town, but to me it was a terrible thing to see my mother and father retreating and leaving me in this alien environment. I thought, 'Oh, no, I can't stay here', but I wouldn't say so. I knew I'd got to work as my parents couldn't afford to keep me.

The first person I saw was another young girl just about my own age. She told me she was Mary, the under-housemaid, and she said, 'I'll help you upstairs with your tin trunk.' Help me upstairs! I'd never seen anything like it! I never thought there could be so many stairs in a house.

From the basement until you got up to two floors below the attics there were back stairs for the servants to use, so that you never interfered with 'Them', and 'They' never saw you running up and down the stairs or anything. And of course the back stairs were very different from the front stairs. They only had linoleum on them, the same as our stairs had at home.

It was a good job I didn't have many clothes because I don't know how we would have got this tin trunk up to the room.

When we did get there I said to Mary, 'What do I do now?' She said, 'The first thing you do is to change straight away into your uniform and come downstairs. And by the way,' she said, 'you'll have to do something about that hair of yours, you can't come down like you are.' I had very long hair because it was before the days of people having their hair cut off. I'd tried to put it up in a bun to go into service and Mother had helped me to do it, but it was all falling down and I didn't have half enough hairpins. Anyway Mary said, 'I'll help you.' She scraped it all back off my face; I had pulled it forward in an effort to make myself attractive. But Mary said, 'The cook won't let you have your hair like that. When you've got your cap on none of your hair must show in the front at all.' So she scraped it all back and she screwed it in a bun at the back, and not only did she use all the hairpins I had but she gave me a dozen of hers as well. I felt like a pincushion at the back. When I put my hand up I could feel nothing but hairpins, and when I looked in the glass at my face with not a scrap of hair showing, I thought I looked hideous. Little did I know I was going to look hideous the whole time I worked there, so really it made very little difference starting off like that.

I got the uniform on, and oh how I hated it! As a kitchen maid I had to wear this uniform morning and afternoon. I didn't change into black like the upstairs servants did. It was a blue uniform, not navy blue, a sort of between navy and saxe blue. Then I put on one of those wide aprons with a bib and straps over the back that buttoned on to the ones that went round your waist, and then the wretched cap. I hated that cap until I got to be a cook, and I never wore a cap then. I had a battle royal with one woman I worked for over it, but I'd never wear a cap as a cook.

When I was dressed Mary said, 'Now we'll go down to the kitchen.' When we got down there it was teatime for the servants. That's one meal the kitchen maid doesn't have to get, the under-housemaid gets it.

# 10

I THINK ONE of the worst ordeals was meeting all the servants, although compared with some of the other houses I worked in later, there weren't so many. There was a butler; a parlour-maid instead of a footman; two housemaids – upper and under; a governess; and a gardener/chauffeur; the cook and me.

The first thing I was shown before I sat down and had my tea was a list of the kitchen maid's duties. When I looked at this list I thought they had made a mistake. I thought it was for six people to do.

Kitchen maid's duties – rise at five-thirty (six o'clock on Sundays), come downstairs, clean the flues, light the fire, blacklead the grate (incidentally, when you blackleaded the grate you didn't have nice tins of liquid polish, you had a hard old lump of blacklead, which before you went to bed at night you had to put into a saucer with water and leave soaking all night before it would assume any kind of a paste to do the grate with. I didn't know this, and nobody bothered to tell me. I tried to do it next morning with this lump; I thought you had to rub it on the stove. No one told me anything. Why people should assume I knew, I don't know), clean the steel fender and the fire-irons (that steel fender, without exaggerating, was all of four foot long, with a tremendous shovel, tongs, and poker all in steel, which all had to be done with emery paper), clean the brass on the front door, scrub the steps, clean the boots and shoes, and lay the servants' breakfast. And this all had to be done before eight o'clock. The things that were written down to do after breakfast throughout the day, well, I'd never seen such a list in my life.

So what with the uniform, the cap, my hair, and the list of duties, well, when Mary said, 'Come and have your tea and meet all the servants,' I felt that life couldn't hold anything worse for me. I was in the lowest pit. I thought, 'How could my mother let me come here and tell me that things were better now, you didn't have to work so hard, you've got more free time, and people think more of you?'

So I went into the servants' hall, and when I say I met the other servants, don't think I was introduced to them. No one bothers to introduce a kitchen maid. You're just looked at as if you're something the cat brought in. One of them said 'She looks hefty enough'. It was just as well I was hefty, believe me.

I sat down and had my tea, but how I ate it with all these servants looking at me, I don't know. Fortunately my mother – and father – had always been very insistent on table manners. We were never allowed to sit anyhow at the table, we always had to use the right things.

I hadn't yet met the cook; she was out, she'd gone to see a film. The cook had a lot more free time than anyone else; the cook could go out any afternoon she liked, so long as she was back in time to cook the dinner at night. Naturally, she was the one I was most keen on meeting because it was with her a large part of my life would have to be spent.

Mary told me that Mrs McIlroy – a Scots cook she was – was quite a pleasant person, but I took that with a grain of salt because Mary wasn't under her, so it didn't make a lot of difference what Mary thought about her.

After tea I went and had a look at the kitchen. That was enough to strike a final note of depression.

Occupying one whole side of the kitchen was the range, and I stood and looked at the thing in amazement. We had a kitchen range at home, but my mother never cooked on it, she had a gas stove. But there was no gas stove in this kitchen, only this tremendous range, which was to become to me, although I didn't know it at the time, a nightmare. It had ovens each side of it, one big and one small, and it had been so polished up with blacklead by the previous kitchen maid that you could almost see your face in it. It never looked like that after I did it somehow, I don't know why. As the cook said, some people can polish and some can't. In front of it was the steel fender, and that also was polished to a silvery brightness.

Opposite it was a dresser with great big cupboards on the lower half of it and five shelves on the other half, all plain white wood. Not the small kind of dresser we had in our own little kitchen at home, but one that could take a whole dinner set, and when I say a whole one I don't mean the kind you buy now which are really only halves; a hundred and twenty-six pieces of china were ranged on the shelves, and on the flat part of it, which was the top of the cupboards, were an enormous soup tureen, vegetable dishes, and sauce boats. It was my job, written down in my duties, to take this whole lot down once a week and wash every single piece of it, and scrub the dresser.

On the third wall there were two doors; one led into servants' hall. It used to be quite an enjoyable occupation when we were sitting in there having our meals to look at the legs of the passers-by in the street and to give a face to the legs. If you saw a fat pair of legs go by you would say, 'Fifty if she's a day', and somebody would say, 'No, not her, she's got duck's disease or water on the knees.'

Incidentally, I never know why they called it a servants' hall. It didn't resemble a hall, it was just a room. But everywhere I went the room the servants sat in was called a servants' hall.

The other door led into the butler's pantry. Although it was called a pantry it was not a place where food was kept. There were two sinks, one to put the soap in to wash all the silver, and the other with plain water to rinse it and to wash all the glasses. The butler and the parlourmaid between them did all the silver and all the glassware; not the knives, that came into the kitchen maid's province.

Another door in the fourth wall led into a long passage from the back door to the kitchen – a huge place, all stone-flagged. In this passage, hanging on the wall, was a long row of bells with indicators above them to show where they rang from, and it was my job every time a bell went to run full tilt out into the passage to see which bell it was. We had whistles in the house. You pulled a plug out in the wall and whistled up to the various rooms to see if you could catch anybody to tell them they were wanted. If you didn't run like mad out into the passage, the bell would stop ringing before you got there, and you had no idea whether it was from the blue room, the pink room, first bedroom, second bedroom, fifth bedroom, drawing-room, or dining-room. So you would come back to the cook and say, 'I don't know which bell it was.' 'You must be quicker,' she'd say, 'otherwise all hell will be let loose upstairs.' But what could you do? If you were in the middle of something you couldn't drop it straight away. I was always in trouble over these bells at first, but at last I mastered the art, and nobody shot out quicker than I did when they rang.

The kitchen floor itself was all stone, not nice shiny stone flags that you see new, but just sort of large bricks. They had to be scrubbed every day. Down the whole length of the room was the kitchen table; a heavy great thing on four of the hugest square legs I have ever seen, and it had been scrubbed to a whiteness that would have been the envy of any washing powder today, although we only had soap and soda then. That was the cook's table which, Mary informed me, I had to set out.

She said to me, 'You know how to set a cook's table, don't you?' I said, 'Yes, I know how to put things out for cooking,' but little did I know how to set it out, really and truly.

That same evening, about six o'clock, Mrs McIlroy, the

cook, came in, and a very pleasant person she seemed. She came up to me and actually shook hands, which was more than anybody else had done.

She was a woman about fifty, a Scotswoman, rather short with grey hair, very down-to-earth type of person, rather plain, but she had such a pleasant personality that you never really noticed how plain she was.

Later on, after I had got to know her better, I said, 'Mrs McIlroy', the Mrs was just a courtesy title; most cooks, if they had not married and if they were a Miss and they were getting on in years, were called Mrs not only by the people they worked for, but by the other servants as well. 'Mrs McIlroy,' I said, 'I wonder you've never got married,' and I piled the old flattery on because I found it always paid off, especially when you happened to be under the person, 'you've got such an attractive personality', nearly choking myself when I was saying it. She said, 'Well, it's like this, my girl. When I was about twenty-five I looked in the mirror and I said to myself, "Girl, a good plain cook you've decided to be, and a good plain cook you're going to be all your life. It's certainly sure you're plain and it's certainly sure no one is going to want to marry you." That's how I found it was too.'

That first evening after she'd introduced herself she said, 'Well, girl, we've got to get on with it. You'll lay up my table, won't you?' 'Oh yes,' I said, and she went up to her room.

All I put out was a knife, a fork, and a spoon, the flour, the salt, and a sifter. I thought that was all she'd need for cooking the dinner. Luckily for me, Mary came out while I was doing it, and after explaining with a fit of giggles that my idea of laying out a cook's table was hopeless, she said, 'I'll show you how to do it. I'll show you before Mrs McIlroy comes back, not that she will grumble, but she might start laughing when she sees what you've put out.' Mary began. There were knives of all kinds, all shapes and sizes, big long carving knives, small knives for paring fruit, pallet knives, bent knives for scraping out basins with, and then metal spoons, not the ordinary type – they were like a kind of aluminium-coloured spoon – huge ones, about six of them. The largest ones had the measures on them, from ounces right up to dessert-spoonfuls. She put out two sieves, a hair sieve and a wire sieve, and a flour sifter, and an egg whisk. Naturally, there were no electric whisks in those days. In fact, there weren't even the ones with the wheels, you had a kind of wire contraption that you had to beat by hand. Then there were two kinds of graters, one fine one for nutmegs, and one to do the breadcrumbs on; there was a big chopping board and a small chopping board, three or four kinds of basins, paprika pepper and cayenne pepper, ordinary salt, pepper, and vinegar. Half the table was covered with these things. All these implements had to be laid out twice a day; for lunch, although the lunch was only three courses, and for dinner again at night, when there were five or six.

When I saw all that I said to Mary, 'She can't use all those things.' 'Oh,' she said, 'you've not seen anything. By the time dinner starts in this house you will be running around wiping things because cook used them once and she wants them again. She uses some of these things two or three times in the course of preparing the meal.' It turned out to be true.

# 11

THE AMOUNT of food that came into that house seemed absolutely fabulous to me, the amount of food that was eaten and wasted too. They often had a whole saddle of mutton. You don't see saddles very much now but they were gorgeous things. And sirloins. Sometimes with the sirloin they would only eat the undercut and the whole top was left over, so we used to have that for our dinner. Even so, we couldn't eat everything and a lot got thrown away. When I used to think of my family at home where we seldom had enough to eat, it used to break my heart.

The milkman called three times a day – at half past four to five in the morning he would leave some milk, then he would come round again at ten o'clock with more milk and any other orders that you wanted. Naturally, he carried cream and eggs with him, but if you wanted butter or cakes which he sold, or anything like that, he came yet again at about two o'clock in the afternoon.

I've never seen such milk and cream and eggs. Pints of

cream nearly every day was nothing in that household, even when they weren't entertaining, when there was only Mr and Mrs Clydesdale and the young daughter and the governess. When I was first there the milk was served from a great big churn with a handle. Not the kind of churns they roll around on railway stations, or did do, but a churn he carried in his hand. But very soon after that it did change to bottles, which was very much cleaner, of course, because the cans used to smell.

Most of the shopping was ordered from a grand shop in Hove, like Fortnum and Mason's, only you had to be a member to use it. I suppose in a way it was a rich man's Co-op. I don't know if you got a dividend.

They had departments for everything; greengrocery, butchery, cakes, and ordinary groceries.

Mrs Clydesdale would come down about ten o'clock and give cook her menus for the day, and if Mrs McIlroy wanted anything she hadn't already in, she would just ring up and ask them to send it around. That's all you had to do with tradesmen in those days. Just ring them up. In fact, the butcher and the greengrocer would come round for orders when they thought cook knew what she wanted for the day, and in less than half an hour they would be back with it.

Fish we never had from them. A man used to come up from the beach, bringing the fish in a bucket filled with sea water, still alive. I used to dread having to see to these fish because when I cut their heads off they jumped and squirmed.

One day he brought up a giant plaice, and when I laid it on the board to chop its head off it jumped right up in the air and its sharp fin made a wide scratch right down my nose. Mary looked at me and said, 'Whatever have you done to your nose?' I said, 'A fish flapped up and scratched me.' It was a long time before I heard the last of that. I never tried the same thing again. I used to get the heavy steel poker and hit them on the head with it. I never found out where the vulnerable part of the fish was, but my way worked all right.

The same fisherman used to bring lobsters up alive. I used to put them in a bowl in a larder. It was a huge larder, not just a place with shelves all round, it was like a room on its own, with a heavy slated floor and slated shelves which were stone cold even in the summer.

I used to put these lobsters in a bowl on the floor, but when I went in at night to get them for dinner they were never inside it; they had got out and were crawling around. I used to pick them up, often getting a nip for my pains. I never knew where the safest part was to get hold of them.

I hated dropping them into boiling water. Mrs McIlroy said they were killed the instant they touched the boiling water, but were they? I never used to believe they were because I am sure they used to give a terrible squeak as I dropped them in.

Mrs McIlroy had no 'arrangement' with the shops, but nevertheless when she paid the quarterly bills some little gift would often be given to her, and at the end of the year quite an appreciable discount, as they called it, was paid to her.

It was the cook who really chose the shops, so when she

went in they laid the red carpet down for her. Because, although ours wasn't such a large staff, the food was of a very high quality. So that, apart from her salary, any cook could count on a regular bonus from the shops at which she dealt.

But to get back to my daily round. I found that what I had thought was work for six was, in fact, work for one, and that one was me from now on.

Up I got at five-thirty, dragged myself downstairs, and presented myself to the kitchen range. I lit it, cleaned it, and lit the fire in the servants' hall.

Then I'd tear upstairs to do the front door, which was all white paint and brass – a thankless task, particularly in the winter, for when I'd got it all bright and shiny the wind from the sea tarnished it again. So by the time Madam saw it, it was something to find fault with.

Then there were fourteen wide stone steps to be scrubbed. Back downstairs again, and there was Mary waiting with all the boots and shoes.

I remember the first morning. She said, 'Carrie' (that was the head housemaid) 'says she hopes you know how to clean boots and shoes.' 'Well, of course I do,' I said. After all, I'd done them at home. But I didn't know how to do them the way they wanted them done.

The Reverend, he used to wear boots all day; black boots in the week and brown boots on Sundays. In the evenings he changed into black patent shoes. Madam wore black or brown, often both during the course of the day. Then there were the governess's, and Leonora's. These I did and I thought they looked very nice indeed. Well, the toes shone anyway.

When Mary came down for them she said, 'Oh, they won't do. They won't do at all.' I said, 'What's the matter with them? They look all right to me.' 'All right,' she said, 'I'll take them up if you like but Carrie will only sling them back at me.'

About two minutes afterwards down she came again and said, 'It's like I said, they won't do. You haven't done the insteps.' 'The insteps?' I said. 'I never knew you had to clean underneath the shoes.' So I did that, gave them another polish, and Mary took them up again.

Seconds later back she came and said, 'You haven't done the bootlaces.' I said, 'Haven't done the bootlaces!' 'Don't you know?' she said. 'You have to iron all the bootlaces, take them all out and iron them.' I thought she was joking. 'Iron the bootlaces?' I said. She said, 'Yes.' You see in those days they weren't the narrow little bootlaces they are now, they were quite half an inch wide. In fact Mrs Clydesdale's and Leonora's were nearly an inch wide.

So I had to take the laces out of the shoes and iron them. Of course, there were no electric irons, just flat irons. They had to be heated in front of the fire and that took nearly a quarter of an hour. Never in all my life have I seen such a footling procedure.

After that I had to clean the knives because there were no stainless ones in those days. I did this with a large round knife-machine; it had three holes into which I shook the knife-powder, a sort of emery powder. Then I put a knife into each of these holes and turned the handle.

I felt like an organ-grinder. Indeed the whole business became a musical affair – I sang as I turned.

> *'A young man stood within the court,*
> *'Twas some poor girl he had made sport,*
> *He heaved a bitter, bitter sigh*
> *When she upon him cast her eye.'*

(By then three knives were done, and I'd put another three in.)

> *'She sued him for a thousand pounds*
> *For breach of promise on these grounds.*
> *But on the day they should have wed*
> *He did a dive from church and fled.'*

(Next three).

> *'Not au revoir but goodbye, Lou,*
> *I've got a better girl than you.*
> *She loves me for myself you bet,*
> *And we have bought a basinet.'*

(Then the last three would go in for the last verse.)

> *'The jury looked at him and grinned.*
> *The Judge could see she'd got him pinned.*
> *She won the day, but don't forget*
> *She hasn't got the money yet.'*

By now it was time to take Mrs McIlroy a cup of tea. Then I laid up breakfast in the servants' hall, and at eight o'clock the staff had their meal.

After we'd had our breakfast it was time for Mrs McIlroy and me to cook for upstairs.

Like most of the meals this was very different from what we had. Mrs Clydesdale thought only about our nourishment, so we used to have things like herrings and cod and stews and milk puddings, but none of these nourishing foods ever found their way upstairs. So I was forced to the conclusion that even their internal organs differed from ours, inasmuch as what nourished us did them no good at all.

There were always economies which had to be made. During my years in domestic service I noticed that all economies began with the servants and always ended with them too.

The breakfasts they had upstairs were always huge, whether they had visitors or whether they didn't; there were bacon and eggs, sausages, kidneys, either finnan haddock or kedgeree – not one or two of these things but every one.

I couldn't help thinking of my poor father and mother at home. All they had was toast. And all this food going up to them, who never worked. I just couldn't help thinking of the unfairness of life.

If I said so to Mrs McIlroy she couldn't see it, she just accepted her lot. She thought there ought to be the people who had the money and the people who didn't. 'Because,' she said, 'if there weren't the people who had the money, what would there be for people like us to do?' 'But,' I said, 'couldn't it be equalled out more – more equitably – for them not to have so much, and for us to have a little bit more? Why do you and I have to work in this dungeon with the barest of comforts while they have everything upstairs? After all,' I said, 'don't forget, Mrs McIlroy, our board and our lodging is part of our wages. The two pounds a month that I have in money is supposed to be supplemented by the board and lodging. If the lodging is of the kind that Mary and I have in that attic, and the food is meagre, and the outings are so small,' I said, 'how are we getting an equitable wage?'

Even at that early stage I used to think about these things. Maybe through my father, because the inequalities of life used to cause him a lot of heartache. Mother didn't take the same notice. So long as she could just have a drink now and again and give us enough to eat, which she could in the summer, she didn't seem to mind so much, but Dad felt these things more.

After breakfast had been washed up we started preparing lunch.

Lunch, according to Mrs McIlroy, was a very simple meal. Soup, fish, cutlets, or a grill, and a sweet. One of the things she taught me was how a dish should be sent up. For instance, when it was cutlets, she would mash the potatoes and roll them in egg and breadcrumbs, in little balls, slightly larger than walnuts, and then she would arrange them in a pyramid on a silver dish and the cutlets would stand on end all round with a little white frill on each bone and parsley at intervals around the dish. It really looked most attractive.

For us the main meal was the middle-day meal because at night we just had anything that was left over. Although it was our main meal I noticed we never got three courses, we only had meat and sweet; fairly substantial, but not cutlets or fillet steak or anything like that. When it was fish, it was herrings or cod. Still, there was always enough of it, and as I'd never been used to luxurious living, I always ate anything there was.

# 12

THE MAIN meal was always at night, even when there were only Mr and Mrs Clydesdale, their little girl Leonora, and the governess. These last two had their meals in a separate place altogether except on Sundays, when Leonora was allowed to have her meals with her parents. It was always five, sometimes six courses.

It would start with soup of some kind. Mrs McIlroy was very good at making clear soup. We used to get lovely bones from the butcher which she'd stew in a saucepan on the side of the range all day long with herbs in a little muslin bag, and with a carrot, onion, swede, or turnip. Towards the end of the evening she would take all these out and put in eggshells, not the eggs themselves, just the shells, and vigorously whisk it. Every bit of scum used then to come to the top, and it was my job – and a jolly long job it was too – to skim everything off the top. When I'd got as much off as I could with a spoon, I had to get greaseproof paper and lay it gently on top of the liquid so that it kept on absorbing the fat.

Sometimes I had to lay over a dozen pieces. By then the soup was clear – a pale, faintly golden colour, but as clear as water.

Sometimes it was tomato soup; of course it wasn't out of tins. No soup was out of tins. For tomato soup again there was the stock – we always had a stockpot going. When I got to be cook I did too. Every single bone that was left over from saddles of mutton, or legs of mutton, or sirloin, every bone or every bit of vegetable we didn't use went into the stockpot. For tomato soup Mrs McIlroy used to melt butter (we never used margarine; everything was butter) over the side of the range, so that it just gently melted. She then thickened it with flour, added the stock, the tomatoes cut in half, and the whole lot was mixed until it thickened. Then I had to put it through a wire sieve. A long job it was too, getting all the pips and skins out of the way.

Mushroom soup was another speciality of Mrs McIlroy's. Made rather similarly, except that the mushrooms had to be put through a hair sieve. She said that if you put them through a wire sieve you got tiny little pieces because they were so soft they went through too easily.

A hair sieve was like a wire sieve in shape, but instead of being covered in wire, it was covered in very fine hair – it felt like horse hair but yet it seemed a lot finer than that.

About five minutes before Mrs McIlroy was going to send it up, she would put a whole gill of cream into the tureen – a great big china one with a ladle with a long handle. It always used to remind me of that saying about the devil and the spoon. I used to say, 'They're supping with the devil all right, up there with that spoon.'

If there was any left Mrs McIlroy used to give it to me because there wasn't enough to share among everyone. I was always hungry, and I used to eat everything there was to eat. She used to say, 'You'll go off your food in the finish, you do when you're with it.' I never did. I think it was the years of semi-starvation when I was a child. Even now I can eat anything there is to eat.

Often there was an entrée for the next course. Sometimes Mrs McIlroy used to do pieces of chicken in aspic jelly. She used to make her own aspic jelly, with stock and gelatine; nowadays it's all bought ready made. If they'd had chicken the night before and there was some left over, I used to cut it up in small pieces and Mrs McIlroy would make this aspic with the gelatine, the stock, and the seasonings, place these pieces of chicken into it, and then put it in an icebox. We didn't have any refrigerators, of course.

We used to have a big metal galvanized box, and every morning the iceman would come around with a large lump of ice, which I put in a tray on the top of the box. The food that needed chilling was put in there. Having a larder that was practically all made of slate and in the basement into the bargain, very little food went bad. In any case, nobody tried to keep food, it was brought fresh in every day.

Then would come the fish course. Sometimes salmon if salmon was in season, sometimes lemon soles, sometimes turbot, each with the appropriate sauce; hollandaise, tartare, or mayonnaise. It was my job to make the mayonnaise sauce.

And what a job it was too. I never thought I'd get it right. First I would drop one egg yolk in a basin, then add olive oil, one spot at a time, only one spot, and I kept stirring and stirring and stirring, until I got a lovely thick yellow mixture, rather like custard. But if I tried to hurry it – to put the olive oil in a bit quick – the whole thing curdled and I had to throw it away and start all over again. I threw away a lot of mayonnaise sauce in my time!

Then came the main course, sometimes a round of beef, sometimes, if they had visitors, it would be a whole saddle of mutton, sometimes just a leg of lamb.

Mrs McIlroy used to make a beautiful sort of glaze. I really never knew how she did it. You can buy it out of bottles now, but she used to make her own out of a kind of burnt sugar. It used to melt and go a lovely toffee colour, and she would spread this over the leg or saddle before she sent it up; it really looked glorious.

Then the sweet. This could be anything, but was nearly always something cold; perhaps a chocolate whisk, which used to be made with grated chocolate, eggs, and castor sugar; or perhaps fruit, fresh fruit with sugar boiled down into a syrup and tipped on top of it; perhaps a compote of oranges, or a compote of bananas; not always a savoury because the Reverend Clydesdale wasn't very fond of savouries. He sometimes liked sardines or anchovies on toast. Nothing too fancy.

Then came cheese and coffee. That was their dinner.

What we had at night were the left-overs of the day before or a macaroni cheese or welsh rarebit. It wasn't Mrs McIlroy's fault, she wasn't allowed to give us more. Some of the maids used to moan like mad and say they never got enough to eat. I didn't moan, but I used to feel it wasn't fair.

Although their dinner at night wasn't until eight, I had to get things ready for Mrs McIlroy before six o'clock because as well as laying out the table, everything she cooked was prepared by hand. For instance, if she was making a cheese soufflé, which was a thing they were very fond of, Mrs McIlroy used to do it with Parmesan cheese because it's a lighter cheese in texture and in weight than the ordinary kind. Now today, of course, you can buy Parmesan cheese ready grated in bottles; in those days you had a lump of it, and believe me, it was as hard as a rock, and I used to have to grate this on the fine side of the grater. That took quite a long time, and some of my knuckles at first.

If it was horseradish sauce, that had to be done by hand too. Grating horseradish is far worse than doing onions. The tears used to stream from my eyes. I used to dread having to do it. If it was creamed spinach, this had to be put through the sieve and that was another long chore.

The worst job of the lot was when they had minced beef cake. The raw beef, generally a fillet, had to go through the mincer. This wasn't easy. But then I had to get it through a wire sieve, still raw, so you can imagine how long this took. I thought it was impossible when I first tried, but I found I could do it if I kept on long enough.

The sieved beef was then mixed with herbs and a yolk of egg, tied up in a piece of muslin, and dropped into a little stock and simmered for not more than twenty minutes. So that when it was cut open the steak was still more or less raw, but because it was so fine after going through the sieve, it tasted as if it had been cooked until it was tender. It was a marvellous thing but it took a lot of work.

If they were serving game they had potato crisps with it. Nowadays everybody buys potato crisps in bags or tins, but in those days they had to be done by hand. First of all you peeled the potatoes, then you got a clean tea cloth and laid it out full length on the table and sliced the potatoes by hand so thinly that when you held them up you could see right through them. They were like little rashers of wind. You laid each one separately on the cloth. Then you covered them up with another cloth until they dried. Then you melted fat – lard, not dripping because that was too coloured. (We used to get our lard not in half-pounds, but in whole bladders as they used to call them. They were about the size of a rugby football and about the same shape.) You melted a portion of that in a frying-pan, a very deep one, and when it was boiling and blue smoke came off, you dropped these crisps in, one by one, because if you dropped two in at a time they stuck together; they wouldn't separate out. By the time you got the last one in, the first ones were already cooked, so it was one mad rush to drop them in and get the first lot out again. If you left them a minute longer than you should, instead of being pale, golden crisps, they were dark brown chips, as hard as rocks.

When my mother asked me if I'd learnt much cooking I said, 'No, Mum, there isn't any time', but I suppose I really was absorbing knowledge, because when I took my first place as a cook, I was amazed at the things I found I could do.

# 13

ALTHOUGH MR CLYDESDALE had a gardener/chauffeur and a car of his own, on two mornings a week he used to have a hackney cab call at the door, with a decrepit old horse in the shafts. It looked as if it should have been in the knacker's yard. It was driven by an elderly man called Ambrose Datchet.

This Ambrose Datchet, so he told me when he used to talk to me (which wasn't very often because he mainly talked to the cook), had been a gardener in a large household, far bigger than my mother or I ever worked in. It had two stewards, two chefs, seven footmen, six housemaids, and over twenty-eight gardeners, of whom he was one. He started off as a hallboy, but he didn't like working inside, and when he saw the footmen, who always had to walk around in uniform and wear white gloves and even wigs, he said he couldn't stick that life, so he went to the outside and became a gardener.

I used to hear him talking to Mrs McIlroy about the things

that used to go on in this great big place where he worked. I listened all agog – you know how it is when you hear anything you think you're not supposed to hear, you think it's something out of this world. Well, according to this Ambrose Datchet, the most outrageous affairs used to go on in this household, and strangely enough, not so much among the women servants as between the footmen and stewards and the people upstairs; not only the people who owned the house but the visitors too. Once I heard Mrs Mellroy say, 'Not her ladyship!' Ambrose Datchet said, 'I saw it with my own eyes.' So Mrs McIlroy said, 'What, with her?' 'Her, and with him too,' he said. 'He was a very handsome young man.' I gathered it was one of the footmen having an affair with both the lady and the master of the house.

Mind you, what Mr Ambrose Datchet saw with his own eyes must have meant he had eyes at the back of his head, because if I heard him say, 'I saw it with my own eyes' once, I must have heard him say it a hundred times.

I remember a story he told me once about a raw country girl who went into service – it was her very first place – and the lady said to her, 'Elsie, I like my breakfast at eight o'clock in the morning.' So Elsie said, 'Oh, that's all right, Madam. If I'm not down, don't wait for me.'

When Ambrose Datchet came back from these outings with Mr Clydesdale he used to be allowed to come down in the kitchen. If it was the summer he'd have a glass of lemonade, if it was the winter he would have a cup of cocoa. He would sit there and jaw to Mrs McIlroy and sometimes to Mr Wade, the butler.

When it was time to go, he used to walk right through the kitchen into a sort of yard place at the back. I thought at first he was going to talk to our gardener/chauffeur, but when he came back Mrs McIlroy used to say, 'Hello, Ambrose. Been to shake hands with your best friend?' I hadn't the faintest idea what they were laughing at, but the fact that they looked at me made me go as red as a beetroot. After it was explained to me, I used to laugh too. Mrs McIlroy, although she looked a bit prim, she could say things with the best of them.

Most mornings Mrs Clydesdale went out for her constitutional. I used to dread it when she came back because she used to scrutinize the front door. The brass on that front door was something too terrible for words. The door handle was all convoluted and the Brasso would get into the cracks of it, and there was a tremendous knocker, the shape of a big gargoyle. That was all nooks and crannies, and there was a big brass letterbox too. The doorstep was also all brass. Some mornings when it was bitterly cold and my hands were covered in chilblains, I used to skip a bit. I didn't leave anything showing as far as I knew, but she could usually find something.

If the bell used to ring two minutes after she came in, I knew what it was for. The parlourmaid would come down and say to me, 'Madam has sent down a message that she wants to speak to Langley' (that was me) 'in the morning room.'

My legs used to feel like rubber at the very thought of going up there, because I knew what she was going to say; I knew it was about the front door. She would start off with a very ambiguous remark, 'Langley, whatever happened to the front door this morning?' Well, she could have equally meant that it looked a picture as that it wasn't done very well, but I knew perfectly well what she meant. Then she would go on to say, 'Langley, you have a good home here, you have good food and you have comfortable lodgings and you're being taught a trade, and in return I expect the work to be done well.' By this time I was in tears, what with feeling so inferior. I was only fifteen years old; by the time I'd been in service a bit longer, I got much harder, and it never used to make me turn a hair when they said these kind of things to me.

When I got back downstairs, even Mrs McIlroy used to be sympathetic. She'd say, 'Oh well, never mind, girl, just remember their bodies have to function the same way as ours do.' I couldn't see what difference that made, and in any case their bodies could function in comfort. All we had was a lavatory in the basement which was the haunt of all the fauna, hairy spiders, blackbeetles, and every other kind of insect.

Many a night Mary, who used to share the attic bedroom with me, used to wake up and want to go to the lavatory. She was frightened of going down all those stairs alone, so she used to wake me up to go with her. We used to creep down, trying to avoid the stairs that creaked – just like criminals. As a matter of fact, I reckon Mrs Clydesdale would have thought we were criminals, because she would have said that servants should be as regular in their habits as they were in anything else, and not go to the lavatory in the night.

One morning when Mr and Mrs Clydesdale were out, Mr Wade came down and asked Mrs McIlroy if she could spare me for a bit.

Mrs McIlroy and Mr Wade were quite friendly, although Mrs McIlroy always thought Mr Wade had a secret in life. Later on, when I had been there some months, he came home 'drunk to the wide', and he was found wearing one of the Reverend's suits. He got the sack there and then. When we went into his bedroom at the back of the butler's pantry, we found a cupboardful of empty whisky bottles. Maybe that was his secret.

Anyway, this particular morning, when Mr Wade came down and asked if she could spare me, Mrs McIlroy said, 'Why?' 'To see the ten o'clock totterers,' he said. 'The ten o'clock totterers, Mr Wade?' 'Yes,' he said. Mrs McIlroy said, 'All right, I can spare her for half an hour,' so we went upstairs, opened the front door and looked.

Up and down Adelaide Crescent were the cars with the smartly uniformed chauffeurs. They wore knee breeches and shiny boots, peak caps, and white gloves. Some of the uniforms were grey, some green, some blue. The chauffeurs stood rigidly to attention beside their cars, ready for when their employers came out.

Almost on the stroke of ten the Crescent sort of sprang into action. It started at the house next but one to ours. The door opened and out came an old gentleman. He was helped down the steps by the butler, then came the old lady on the arm of the housemaid, the under-housemaid carrying a footstool and a horrible old-looking lap dog. The pair were ushered into the car, the footstool was arranged under the old gentleman's feet, and the dog was tenderly placed on the old lady's lap. The chauffeur leaned in and carefully wrapped a rug around both of them. No wind must blow upon them (though goodness knows, some years after that the bitter winds of adversity blew all around them), and off they went. This scene was repeated all around the Crescent. These were the ten o'clock totterers.

Then Mr Wade said he would show me over the house, because, being a kitchen maid, during all the months I had been there, I had seen nothing except the back stairs. All I had done was to go from the basement to the attic.

What a contrast it was to our domain. Beautiful thick carpets everywhere, all colours, Turkey carpets and Chinese carpets in the morning room, the drawing-room, the dining-room, and the bedrooms. Lovely massive armchairs, great big thick velvet curtains, lovely beds with mattresses so thick that no princess would have felt a pea if she had slept on them, like she did in the fairy tale. Everything reflected the life of ease and comfort.

I thought of our bedroom that was so tropical in the summer, and so freezing cold in the winter, that when we left the water in our wash jugs at night, a layer of ice formed on it, and we had to break that to wash in the morning. We couldn't even have a bath in comfort, all we had was a hip bath. For that we had to carry up every drop of water from the bathroom, two flights below, and carry it down to the lavatory when we wanted to empty it. And with a hip bath, I never knew what to do, whether to get right in, sit in it with my bottom down and my knees up under my chin, or to sit in it with my legs hanging outside. Either way I got stone-cold.

Then I thought about the so-called servants' hall, which

was our sitting-room, really. They had lamps, beautiful reading lamps with lovely shades. The only light we had in our servants' hall was one bulb with a white china shade. The floor was covered in old brown lino, with horrible misshapen wicker chairs which had once graced their conservatory and weren't even considered good enough for that now. Depressing walls that were shiny brown paint halfway up, and a most bilious green distemper for the top half, the barred windows and one table with an old cloth; that was our sitting-room.

Mary and I had the worst bedroom, it's true, because we were the two lowest – but even Mrs McIlroy's was only furnished with the cast-offs from upstairs. The bed was one Leonora had at one time or another and wasn't considered good enough for her now. The bits of rugs were once in their bedrooms. Wherever you looked the difference was accentuated. If only they had made some attempt to furnish ours with a few new things. Why did we always have to have the cast-offs?

One job I particularly hated was when it was the gardener/chauffeur's day off, and I had to take out the horrible little dog of Mrs Clydesdale. It was a pug dog and it was so fat and overfed that it was almost square. It was called Elaine, but I couldn't imagine any Lancelot taking a fancy to that Elaine. I used to walk it up and down Adelaide Crescent, and of course it kept hanging round the trees. All the errand boys – there were hundreds of errand boys in those days – used to whistle after me and say, 'I see you've got your monkey with you, where's your organ?' I loathed that job.

# 14

IN MY FIRST months there I made one mistake after another. I particularly remember one day when I was doing the front door – I was a bit late this particular morning – the newsboy came with the papers. As I went to put them on the hall table, Mrs Clydesdale came down the stairs. I went to hand her the papers. She looked at me as if I were something subhuman. She didn't speak a word, she just stood there looking at me as though she could hardly believe that someone like me could be walking and breathing. I thought, what's the matter? I've got my cap on, I've got my apron on, I've got my black stockings and shoes; I couldn't think what was wrong. Then at last she spoke. She said, 'Langley, never, never on any occasion ever hand anything to me in your bare hands, always use a silver salver. Surely you know better than that. Your mother was in service, didn't she teach you anything?' I thought it was terrible. Tears started to trickle down my cheeks; that someone could think that you were so low that you couldn't even hand them anything out of your hands without it first being placed on a silver salver.

I was so miserable about this that I wanted to go home; it seemed the last straw. I thought, I can't stand domestic service. I don't think I ever felt so wretched before or after that. But I knew I couldn't go home, because we had only three rooms – we lived in the bottom half of a house, two rooms on the ground floor and one in the middle – and since I had come into service, my mother's father had died, and my grandmother had to come and live with us. So now there just wasn't room. I didn't even say anything to my mother about it. What was the good of making them unhappy as well? In any case I think she'd just have said, 'Take no notice.' She'd have been right. That's what you had to do if you wanted to keep any pride at all – just take no notice.

Although we weren't forced to attend church, it was taken for granted that we went at least once on Sunday, preferably in the evening. It interfered less with their comfort if we went in the evening. One day the Reverend asked me if I had been confirmed. I said, 'No, I haven't.' He wanted to know why; so I said, 'Well, my mother didn't bother about it, she never mentioned it to me, and now I'm fifteen I don't think it's worth bothering about.' After all I couldn't see what it had to do with being a kitchen maid whether I was confirmed or not, I mean it made no difference to my work; but of course the Reverend was greatly concerned with my religion and with my moral affairs.

In fact, all my life in domestic service I've found that employers were always greatly concerned with your moral welfare. They couldn't have cared less about your physical welfare; so long as you were able to do the work, it didn't matter in the least to them whether you had back-ache, stomach-ache, or what ache, but anything to do with your morals they considered was their concern. That way they called it 'looking after the servants', taking an interest in those below. They didn't worry about the long hours you put in, the lack of freedom and the poor wages, so long as you worked hard and knew that God was in Heaven and that He'd arranged for it that you lived down below and laboured, and that they lived upstairs in comfort and luxury, that was all right with them. I used to think how incongruous it was when the Reverend used to say morning prayers and just before they were over he'd say, 'Now let us all count our blessings'. I thought, well, it would take a lot longer to count yours than it would ours.

For ever below stairs we were making fun of the Reverend. At the time most of it went way over my head. It must have been because of my parents – bad dirty jokes and things like that had never come into my life. I remember when I was cleaning the vegetables, turnips, and salad, one of the maids looked at what I was doing and said, 'Oh! Turn up and let us.' Everybody went into screams of laughter – but I didn't know what it was all about.

They used to go on about the Reverend and the eight children he had by his first wife. They'd compare him with Catholic clergy who don't get married; and say that they wondered how he could ever get up in the pulpit and talk about the sins of the flesh, with a lot more innuendoes that

I didn't really understand at all. I wasn't naïve; I mean I could see very well that for a clergyman who is supposed to preach about spiritual life, and life hereafter, then to have a tremendous family of eight daughters – well, it wasn't really on, although I suppose in those days eight wasn't such a lot. It was just that he was a clergyman, and then him getting married again in an effort to get a son and heir, and having another daughter, well, you couldn't help laughing. You really felt it served the old thing right. I know now I should have given up the ghost after eight daughters and all that went with it. When I got further on in service, of course, and understood what they were talking about, I used to add my quota to it.

One lacks moral courage, because I did stand for lots of the things I didn't like later on when I was in service. If you didn't do them they thought you were stuck up, and after all you had to work with the servants. Not only work with them, you had to live with them, and almost sleep with them. You shared rooms, so it was up to you to keep on good terms with them. They were your whole life.

# 15

I STAYED FOR a year in Adelaide Crescent. Then I decided that I'd try my luck in London. I'd always heard that it was a marvellous place, and that fortunes were to be made there. Not that I believed the streets were paved with gold, or all that baloney of course, but that there was more opportunity in London than there was in a small provincial town.

When I announced this idea at home, the consternation that reigned with my parents, you'd have thought I'd said I was going to Timbuktu. My mother immediately remembered that she'd read an article in a newspaper about how all young girls disappeared as soon as they got to London and were never heard of again. It was well known, she said, that those women, and by 'those women' of course she meant prostitutes, originally were innocent young girls who'd gone to London in the same way that I was suggesting, and been lured away by promises of easy money and a life of luxury. I remember saying, 'Oh, don't worry, Mum. I'll tell them when I'm standing on the corner that I'm only waiting for a bus.' That didn't console my mother. My father never made much fuss about anything. I can't think why Mum did because I wasn't such a wildly attractive girl that any young man was going to take one look at me and decide that he needed me to decorate his harem. I suppose she thought it was a sort of disintegration of the family. People were much keener on families in those days than they are now.

Anyway, in spite of all her protestations and prognostications, I decided I was fed up with living in Hove, so I got the *Morning Post*, and answered an advertisement for a kitchen maid at a place in Thurloe Square, Knightsbridge.

The wages were an advance on what I had been getting, four pounds a year more. I know it doesn't sound very much now, but of course money did go further in those days.

My mother wanted to come to London with me. 'You'll get lost, you won't find the place.' 'But Mum,' I said, 'I've got a tongue and a voice and two legs, I can talk, I can walk, there's buses and undergrounds.' I'd never been to London before, I didn't know a soul there.

I said, 'I'm sixteen now, and I'm going to do it all on my own.' It made me feel very much superior to my brothers and sisters, especially to my older brother because elder brothers always lord it over you.

The size and dignity of the houses in Thurloe Square frightened me at first. And the interview with the lady of the house, Mrs Cutler, was even more intimidating than the house itself. When I told her my name was Margaret Langley I could see she considered it a highly unsuitable name for a kitchen maid. It was more like the sort of name you'd have if you were going on the stage, not one to work down in the basement with. I could see she thought it should have been Elsie Smith or Mary Jones. They were the sort of names that kitchen maids had. Margaret Langley would be flighty.

That was always the bugbear of people that employed you. They were always so afraid that you were going to be flighty. The parlourmaids often used to tell us that when they were waiting on people at the ladies' 'at homes' which they had once a month, they heard them talking about their servants. That was one of their main topics of conversation. Then they'd say, 'Yes, I had to get rid of her. She was flighty.' You were flighty if you used the slightest little bit of make-up. People didn't use a lot of make-up in those days, but if you used any, or if you had your hair waved, or if you wore coloured silk stockings; brown silk stockings were all right, but if you wore coloured ones, and I mean on your off-duty periods not when you were on, you were flighty, and flighty girls came to bad ends.

I've never been able to understand why, and I still can't. A bad end meant that we, the so-called lower classes, would get ourselves into the family way. I would have thought we were the last people to go in for illegitimate babies, because we had no means of supporting them, and there were not the homes to go to then. Nowadays you're almost encouraged to have them, with the facilities for girls going into homes and having them looked after when they leave there. Things are made so easy and there is no publicity. In those days you were an outcast if you had a baby outside marriage. So why they should have thought we were so ready to kick over the traces I don't know. Perhaps it was because in their heart of hearts they realized our life was so dreary that any young man that would take you out, regardless of what he wanted in exchange for it, was a treat.

I know that I would never have dared kick over the traces – not because I didn't want to, but because I was too dead scared. I hadn't even the faintest idea just how far I could go without any after-effects, if you know what I mean. So I just had to keep to the straight and narrow because I didn't know where the broad path would lead me.

Despite my name my present path was leading me to Mrs Cutler. I felt as if I was being smothered by her and smothered by the room. Everything was in velvet. Velvet was in vogue at that time. The drawing-room curtains were brown velvet, the three-piece suite was brown velvet, the picture frames had a velvet surround, and Mrs Cutler's bosom was draped in purple velvet. She reminded me of Queen Victoria inasmuch as she also would not have been amused. Life was real, life was earnest for people like her. I wasn't the type that Mrs Cutler wanted. She really wanted a London gal. It was always gal to those people.

Nevertheless she decided that she would employ me. She thought I would do. Probably it was my hefty size and good health that got me the job. I certainly needed both.

When I went there I found they had their married daughter living with them and her three children. They, of course, needed a nanny. Not only a nanny but an undernurse, and nursery meals too. Later on in life I never ever took a place where there were nannies and children, and where they had to have separate meals in the nursery.

The nanny would come down with all the airs and graces of a miniature employer, saying what the children wanted and what she wanted. There were always feuds between the nursery and the kitchen. There always were and there always had been. The parlourmaid, the housemaid, and the cook always thought nanny and nursemaid considered themselves better than *they* were, and they did, of course.

They were a sort of liaison between us and the people upstairs. In lots of ways I think it must have been a problem for them. They were more with the people upstairs; they took the children into the drawing-room in the evening before they went to bed, and they sat in the drawing-room with 'Them', and yet of course they weren't of 'Them'. And when they came downstairs they weren't of 'us' either, because we always thought that they were on friendly terms with 'Them' upstairs and that meant that anything we said about 'Them' would be repeated upstairs. Probably it wouldn't have been but that was what it seemed it might be.

The cook, of course, used always to be furious at the nanny coming into the kitchen. The kitchen was the cook's domain. Only the mistress of the house was allowed in it and her only once in the morning to give her orders. The nanny coming and asking 'What is the menu for today, cook?' or 'Mrs' if she was called 'Mrs'. Well, that infuriated the cook to start with, but if the nanny asked for different food for the children, then the feathers really used to fly.

The cook's name in Thurloe Place was Mrs Bowchard, and

she was an absolute old harridan. The other servants in the house were: the kitchen maid, which was me; instead of having a butler or footman – they weren't very keen on men servants in the house, except that Mr Cutler had a valet – there was a parlourmaid and an upper-parlourmaid; upperhousemaid and under-housemaid; the nanny and nursery maid; a chauffeur and a gardener and a gardener's boy. It wasn't a large staff for a house that size, but judging by present-day standards, you really did two people's work, so you can say more or less that there were six people to run the house, because you don't count the nanny.

The cook was sour. Looking back on it now I would say she was soured by the constant stream of kitchen maids that kept coming and going. They never did stay long. You could generally get a job as a kitchen maid; nowadays, of course, they lay the red carpet down for you, but even then there wasn't a queue for the job. The trouble with kitchen maids, to anyone who wasn't a kitchen maid, was that they were always larking about with the tradesmen.

Perhaps it seems as though my life was one long tragedy. It wasn't. I worked jolly hard and I got miserable often, but no one can be fifteen and sixteen years old and be miserable all the time. Like all the kitchen maids I used to lark around with the tradesmen, especially the errand boys. They were one of the notable sights of London, the way they used to go through the streets with a bicycle laden sky-high, whistling all the latest tunes. And they were cheeky little devils.

And the kitchen maids were cheeky, too, and Mrs Bowchard was soured by the constant procession and the cheekiness and larking around. So she made my working life a misery. She was always carping and always complaining. It wasn't that I was more inefficient than the previous kitchen maids, it was just that I was young. It was a condition that I can assure you she did her utmost to rectify. After a day with Mrs Bowchard you didn't feel so very young.

Another thing about Mrs Bowehard was she suffered from a curious complaint which was called 'melegs'. Doctors wouldn't know about it, but it was always 'melegs'. 'Melegs' prevented her doing so many things; melegs wouldn't let her climb all those stairs to the attics where we all slept, so she had to sleep in the basement; melegs wouldn't let her do anything that anyone else could do for her; melegs wouldn't let her sit down and tie up her shoes so I always had to do that. There was nothing I hated more than having to stoop down in the morning, put Mrs Bowchard's shoes on, and tie them up, and stoop down and untie them and take them off at night. I suppose it's a no more menial task than waiting on all the servants at table, but I felt like one of those little boot-blacks out of Dickens. I really did hate having to do that. It wasn't part of my job, but mind you if you've got to work under the cook, you've got to do what she says, otherwise your life's going to be worse than it is.

Mrs Bowchard had a cat. It was an enormous black and white animal, really a handsome cat I suppose you'd call it. She used to call it 'His Lordship', what I called it I won't repeat. I've never been a lover of animals but 'His Lordship' brought out fierce hatred in me. He was such a supercilious-looking animal. Personally, I think that all cats are supercilious. They gaze at you as though you were less than dust. Mind you, it was a very clever cat, I've got to admit that. He used to sleep in the cook's bedroom. He slept under her bed and a quarter to seven every morning without fail when the alarm went off, that cat used to come out from under the bed, go to the door, put his paw up and rattle the door handle; that was the signal for Mrs Bowchard to get out and open the door and let the cat out. When she did that he used to stroll along the passage, come into the kitchen and stand there and gaze at me. He didn't move, he just stood there until he got my eye, and that was the signal that I had to take Mrs Bowchard along a jug of hot water and a cup of tea. It infuriated me. I used to say, 'I wonder the old girl don't give you a note to put in your mouth and bring along for me. Get out of it.' But, do you know, he wouldn't go. If I shooed him to the door he would stand there until he saw me go along with her jug of hot water and cup of tea. It was really clever, even though I didn't feel like that about it then.

Twice a week we used to have a cod's head delivered for this animal, and I had to cook it for him and remove all the bones. Mrs Bowchard would sit gazing at this cat with the most doting expression. '. . . and don't forget,' she'd be saying, 'to take all the bones out, "His Lordship" mustn't get a bone in his throat, must he?' I used to get livid. But I would do it and then I'd put some down on the floor for him, and you know that wretched beast would sometimes just sniff at it and walk away with his tail and nose in the air. Of course if he did it when the cook wasn't there I'd move him even farther away with the toe of my boot. But that animal got so clever that he wouldn't even look or smell that fish if I was on my own. Oh, he was clever.

Mrs Cutler did a lot of entertaining; two or three times a week there would be a dinner party for at least twelve people, sometimes more, and with all the courses, there was never any time to wash up in between. As soon as one course had gone up you were rushing around getting the plates ready and dishing up the other, so that by the end of the dinner I'd be surrounded by everything under the sun; saucepans and plates and dishes, not the silver because the parlourmaids had to do all the silver and the glasses, but I had everything else to wash up. The things would all be piled up in the sink and on the draining-board, and on the floor in the dark dank old scullery.

The sinks were shallow stone ones, a dark grey in colour, made of cement. They were porous, not glazed china or stainless steel like you get now, and the dirty water sort of saturated into them and they stank to high heaven. That washing-up was what you'd call a chore these days. It was a bore too. After I'd done it, and that took some considerable time, there was still the servants' meal to get laid up and later washed up.

There were six or seven of us altogether, and the valet.

Mr Cutler I had very little to do with. I only saw him as a sort of shadowy thing going in and out. He never came down into the kitchen; even if he'd thought about it, it would be as much as his life was worth. He was something in the City. I'm not well up on these peculiar sort of jobs that necessitate your going off in the morning about ten o'clock and coming home about four in the afternoon, but he didn't do anything very strenuous. He used to go off with a rolled-up umbrella. I asked Mrs Bowchard what he did, when she was in a rather more mellow mood than usual. 'Don't ask me,' she said, 'bugger all.' Still I think he was something in the City.

As I say he had little to do with us. His valet of course saw a lot of him. Now you would think that a valet would be a sort of kingpin in a household. I don't know whether it was always the same, but this one seemed so feminine. Whether it's the nature of their job (although valeting is not really an effeminate job), or whether it's because they're in domestic service and they're living so much with females I don't know, but we used to look on him as one of us. Still valets wouldn't have bothered me. I wasn't going to marry into service. And he seemed inordinately old. I suppose he was about forty-five, but when you're only sixteen, forty-five seems like your grandfather. I was only interested in anyone who was likely to be a permanency. One's whole life was devoted to working to that in those days; getting a permanent boyfriend. And anyone in service was out. So I never took a great deal of notice of the valet.

As I say, it was reciprocated. The cook made more fuss of him than anyone else. She quite liked him. But nobody treated him as though he was a man. They all spoke and made jokes with him as if he was a woman. His hands were so soft, and he was so soft spoken, he didn't seem masculine. More like a jelly somehow, to me. I assume of course he could sire children. I presume he was all there, organically speaking. But you couldn't imagine him trying. He wasn't married and he'd got to forty-five. Maybe he never wanted to get married, I don't know. Looking back, I suppose he was perhaps homosexual, but we certainly never knew of it by that name. One vaguely knew that there were men who 'went with men' as the term was phrased in those days, but even so I never knew anything about it, I don't think anybody else did much. If it went on anywhere in our vicinity it would be very much under cover and nobody talked about such things. If anyone had said the word I wouldn't have known what they were talking about.

The boot-hole was the domain of the kitchen maid. I spent a lot of time in there, among the knives and boots. Mind you, nobody ever dreamt of ironing laces in that place.

When I spoke to Mrs Bowchard about putting the iron on, 'Iron the bootlaces,' she said, 'what are you talking about?' I said, 'Well, in my last job I had to take the bootlaces out and iron them.' 'I've never heard such rubbish, don't do it here,' she said. 'If they don't like it you can tell them to get their own bloody bootlaces out and do them.' She did stick up for me in that way.

Anyway, this boot-hole was really a refuge for me from the demands of that old harridan of a cook. She'd never go into it because it was a very low-pitched place and was festooned with spiders' webs. I used to knock them down just for the pleasure of going in the next day and seeing them spun again.

I know you'll laugh at me, but spiders today don't spin the way they used to. They'd spin their webs from wall to wall in the most intricate designs. If Robert the Bruce had been in there, believe me he'd have had an absolute bun day, he wouldn't have known which one to watch to get him up to start all over again.

It used to take me an hour every morning to clean all the boots and shoes, and I used to make them shine like a mirror. I'd got really expert at it by then, I was even congratulated at that place on doing them, but I used to feel a bit like Cinderella sitting in that boot-hole in an old sacking apron and thinking of all the things I would like to do: not that I ever expected any Prince Charming to come along with a glass slipper, I can assure you. After all when you wear size eights you don't expect Prince Charming to come walking round with one that size for you, do you?

# 16

MRS BOWCHARD had a sister in London who was also a cook, and this sister had married a butler and they worked together in the same house. I used to think how awful it was, marrying a butler and then working in the same house still carrying on your jobs of cook and butler.

It's not like being a cook in a house and having your bit of 'how's your father' with the butler. It's not the same with your husband, is it? Legitimate fun never seems quite the same somehow, does it? It doesn't to me anyway, maybe I've got the wrong idea on it, but I've known cooks who've had a lot of fun with butlers. I thought, well, fancy marrying one and for the rest of their life being in domestic service together; talk about a pair in harmony.

Mrs Bowchard's sister and her brother-in-law worked for a Lord something or other, I forget what his name is now, and they used to have their free evening at the same time. Naturally, they had to, otherwise they'd never have any free time together.

On their evening out they used to call round and see Mrs Bowchard. Talk about a busman's holiday, they must have been steeped in domestic service. They must have had it running in their veins instead of blood. Just imagine one evening out a week, and one Sunday a fortnight, coming round to some other domestic service place and having a meal with your sister who is also a cook. If I couldn't have thought of anything better to do on my evening out than that, I'd have shot myself.

After Mrs Bowchard had done the dinner, she, the two visitors, and the valet would retire to her room. I had to serve their dinner in there before I served the rest of the servants in the servants' hall. You can imagine what my life was; the rest of the servants used to moan like mad because their supper was late, but what could I do? In the order of rank the visitors were more important than the parlourmaids and the housemaids.

Mrs Bowchard's brother-in-law, Mr Moffat, was a very large man with a huge ponderous stomach and a double chin. He used to laugh a lot, usually at his own jokes. His laugh used to start down in the pit of his stomach and his being so fat, it used to ripple up in waves until it reached his double chin and that would flap in sympathy with the rest of him. I was fascinated by it.

He was always talking about his job and how important it was. He would say, 'I said to his Lordship', 'I told his Lordship', 'His Lordship consulted me'; honestly, if you listened to Mr Moffat for long you'd think that his Lordship couldn't do a thing, couldn't make a decision without Mr Moffat's advice.

When he was mellowed by the port and cigars – Mr Cutler's port and cigars – he used to get very arch and sort of frivolous. I thought it was a very incongruous trait in a man of his size, and his age too, and with his so-called dignity. He used to say to Mrs Bowchard when he was in one of these moods and I was waiting on them, 'How are we shaping?' (He was referring to me.) 'Are we learning all we can in the way of cooking? Remember the way to a man's heart is through his stomach.' I used to think to myself, I'd get lost looking for your heart. After he'd said this his whole mound of flesh would shake like a jelly as he had another good old laugh. Mrs Bowchard, whose high colour showed that she'd also consumed an amount of Mr Cutler's port, would say, 'Yes, as kitchen maids go, Margaret isn't too useless.' If Mr Moffat was more mellow than usual he'd even speak to me direct. That was a great condescension, a butler who worked for a lord, and who was consulted by a lord, speaking to a kitchen maid direct. I used to feel I was expected to curtsey. He'd say to me, 'Well, my girl, do you like it here?' What could I say with Mrs Bowchard sitting there? I'd have liked to have said, 'It's the lousiest place I've ever been in,' but I didn't dare.

It's funny, you know, when I think of it now, that I didn't dare. Can you see young girls of sixteen now being frightened to say anything? They'd turn round and say, 'Stuff it', and double quick too.

When I didn't answer he used to say, 'Have you a boyfriend? Ah! When I was your age I used to be a one with the girls; as a young footman I used to have many a kiss and cuddle in the footman's pantry.'

When I used to go to bed at night Gladys used to say to me, 'What was old fatty talking about down there?' because she could hear him with his rumble of a laugh. I used to say, 'He was telling me all about when he was young and what a Don Juan he was.' Then she'd say, 'Well, if he was like he is now with his fat belly, it'd just be "take a tip from me," wouldn't it?' then we'd go off into fits of giggles.

Mrs Moffat, as befitted anyone who had Mr Moffat for a husband, was a meek and mild person. I often wondered if she was meek and mild when she had dealings with her kitchen maid. But everything that Mr Moffat said was gospel truth to her. I don't know what Christian name Mr Moffat had but she never used to call him by it. It was always, 'As Mr Moffat said to his Lordship', or, 'When Mr Moffat was serving Lady so and so', or, 'Mr Moffat told John' (that was one of the footmen). It was 'Mr Moffat this', 'Mr Moffat that'. Her whole life was wrapped around Mr Moffat. What personality she had, if she'd ever had any, and presumably she must have had to have attracted him in the first place, unless it was her cooking that appealed to him, was submerged in him so that in a way although Mr and Mrs Moffat came to dinner with Mrs Bowchard, it was only one person – Mr Moffat.

When I was serving I went to Mr Moffat first, and poured him out his port first. He was the kingpin. He was imbued with the importance of the establishment he worked for. You know, I suppose that's what people mean when they say that the servants live for them.

In Mr Moffat's case it really was so, he aligned himself with his Lordship. When his Lordship went out to dinner

Mr Moffat went out to dinner, because in his mind's eye he saw what his Lordship was doing. When his Lordship was presented to noble personalities, Mr Moffat was also presented to them. I could tell that because he told us things in detail that he couldn't possibly have known because he wasn't at the functions. That, of course, was the kind of servant that people really liked, because if you submerged your whole personality in your employers, they were going to get the very best out of you. I think that's why I was never such a good employee because to me they were a means to an end. A means, at the time, of living, and the end was to get out of service as fast as I could.

Living in such close contact with the other servants, a lot of quarrels went on. You can't coop up a lot of females, perhaps it even applies to men, without words passing, and what words too. But it didn't matter how much we servants quarrelled among ourselves, a united front was always presented to them upstairs.

We always called them 'Them'. 'Them' was the enemy, 'Them' overworked us, and 'Them' underpaid us, and to 'Them' servants were a race apart, a necessary evil.

As such we were their main topic of conversation. The parlourmaids used to come down and tell us. It would go something like this. 'You know if I lived in a little country place I wouldn't bother about servants at all, they are only a nuisance to me; they quarrel among themselves, they want more money, and they don't want to work hard, and they don't do the things the way you want them, but there, you see, I have a certain position to keep up and so I must employ them.'

Mrs Cutler certainly looked upon us as necessary evils, so in that house we were always united against 'Them' upstairs. In the opinion of 'Them', we servants must never get ill, we must never dress too well, and we must never have an opinion that differed from theirs. After all it was perfectly obvious, wasn't it, that if you'd only stayed at school until you were thirteen or fourteen, your knowledge was very small in comparison to what they knew upstairs. So if you had to have opinions why not take them from those upstairs who knew more than you did?

It was the opinion of 'Them' upstairs that servants couldn't appreciate good living or comfort, therefore they must have plain fare, they must have dungeons to work in and to eat in, and must retire to cold spartan bedrooms to sleep. After all, what's the point of spending money making life easier and more comfortable for a lot of ungrateful people who couldn't care less what you do for them? They never tried, mind, to find out if we would have cared more by making our conditions good and our bedrooms nice places in which to rest. No, it wasn't worth spending your money because servants never stayed with you, no matter what you did for them. After all was said and done, only 'Them' upstairs needed luxury living, only 'Them' could grace the dining-room table and make witty conversation. I mean there's got to be a stratum of society in which people can move around graciously and indulge in witty conversation, and no one can do this if they work hard. So make life harder for those who work for you, and the less inclined they'll feel for any kind of conversation.

But if 'Them' upstairs could have heard the conversation the parlourmaids carried down from upstairs, they would have realized that our impassive expressions and respectful demeanours hid scorn, and derision.

# 17

MR CUTLER was fond of shooting. He was in Africa for some years and if the trophies in the house were any indication, he spent a great deal of his time shooting things there.

The hall was absolutely festooned with antlers of this and antlers of that, I don't know what the animals were, all I know is that some were curved and some were straight and it was my job to get up and dust them.

Back in England, of course, with there not being the same kind of animals, he shot at birds. I got sick of the sight of grouse and pheasants and partridges. These were sent down from wherever he was shooting as quickly as possible, they were hung until they were high, and high they certainly got believe me.

They used to hang in the basement passage from an iron rod, and many a morning when I came down I would find just a head hanging there and the body on the floor. The maggots had eaten clean through. Then it was considered high enough to cook for their dinner.

It was my job then to pluck them without breaking the skin and then to clean the insides. A foul job; they reeked to high heaven.

When the cook served the pheasant she'd keep the head with all the feathers on it, and the tail feathers, and when the bird went up to the meal its head would be placed at one end and the tail feathers at the other.

Another distasteful job was cleaning the hares he shot. They seemed simply full of blood. I think they must be vampires and live on blood. In the cold weather they used to hang for two weeks at least, and you needed the strength of ten to remove the skin from them.

I used to try and get it off in one go because anything like that, rabbits' skins or hares' skins, were my perks. The rag- and-bone man used to give me ninepence for a hare skin that was pulled straight off without being torn in any way.

The cook, she would never let me wash the hares. I had to get them clean with tissue paper. She said that if you washed hares or washed game of any kind it took the flavour away. She didn't like you washing anything, she always reckoned that you washed the flavour down the sink.

Mrs Bowchard loved cooking jugged hare because of the port wine. This was always sent down into the kitchen when we had jugged hare. The parlourmaid used to bring it from the dining-room, two wineglasses full, but never more than one glass ever went into the cooking. Mrs Bowchard always used to try and drink it secretly so that I could never say afterwards, 'Well, Mrs Bowchard had some of it.' I used to watch out of the corner of my eye. One glass used to go into the jugged hare, the other glass went down Mrs Bowchard's gullet. If she knew I'd seen her she'd say, 'Oh well, it's the cook's perks. Everyone does it.' Perhaps everyone did; I remember doing it myself later.

Still Mrs Bowchard was a very good cook. Cooking was really something in those days because you had unlimited materials. There was none of this business as in the war when they told you how to make a fatless or eggless cake which was the most appalling thing you ever ate in your life; you used vinegar and lard. People just deluded themselves if they thought it was worth eating.

Even nowadays when you see an economic recipe and they say you can't tell the difference from the original, well probably you can't if you've never eaten the original, but if you have there's a vast difference. It's like using margarine instead of butter, the top of the milk instead of cream, having cheaper cuts of meat instead of the best, and having frozen salmon instead of fresh salmon. None of it tastes the same.

The food was marvellous then because it was always fresh even butchers and fishmongers never had things like deep freeze. They used to have a cold room but it didn't freeze things, so that all the food you had was fresh; it had a flavour.

Nowadays they are at their wits' end to put things on the market to put back the flavour into food, the flavour that's come out with freezing. But it can't be done. No one can delude me into thinking that it can be, but of course if you've not had it the old way you don't know the difference.

Today when people talk about their jobs they always

mention the 'fringe benefits'. As I've said cooks used to get fringe benefits from the stores they dealt with. You'd have thought that cast-off clothes might have found their way downstairs, but they didn't. They didn't care to give them to the servants because they wouldn't want you to wear them while you were living in their house, and of course they wouldn't want you to leave so that you could wear them somewhere else. They preferred to give them to societies.

All these people interested themselves in charities, they were all on this board and that board. If you read the papers you would see Lady this, and Mrs that, had a stall here and a stall there.

Mrs Bowchard used to make cakes for the stall Mrs Cutler ran for helping fallen women. Mrs Cutler used to be very keen on helping the fallen women, from a distance. Like a lot of people, she could be generous if she was not involved. It was to charities like this that they used to send their old clothes.

I remember the head parlourmaid being very annoyed once because there was a nice coat with a fur collar which Mrs Cutler had had several years. The head parlourmaid knew that she'd very soon be getting rid of it and she felt sure it would come to her because she'd dropped a few hints which seemed to have had an effect, but no, it was packed up and sent to a charitable institution.

There wasn't very much given away to us. At Christmas, we got presents of cloth to make things with, aprons, and horrible sensible presents.

Although I'd made such a fuss about going there, during

the two years that I stayed in Thurloe Square I saw very little of London. I was always too tired to go and look. Yet before I went I got a book on various aspects of old London. Where people had stayed, like Carlyle, Wells, and Dickens, and I thought how marvellous it would be to walk around and to be able to say that I'd been there, because I was always mad on history and reading.

But I was always too darned tired, I just wanted to go to the films where you could sit in darkness, where it didn't matter that you hadn't dressed up.

On my day off I used to go to the nearest cinema and get all my romance second-hand. It took a lot less energy. I often thought I wouldn't have had the strength if a marvellous lover had swum into my life. I couldn't have done anything about it.

Once a fortnight I used to get a Sunday evening off with Gladys the under-housemaid, and we used to stroll around Hyde Park.

Gladys was a year older than me and she'd lived in London all her life. Her home was in Stepney, she had eight brothers, and ten sisters. She could hardly remember when her mother wasn't having a baby. She told me lurid tales of life in Stepney, the overcrowding that there was, and bugs in the beds, the filth, and the drinking, and the fights on Saturday nights. I thought it was marvellous to listen to, although I wouldn't have wanted to be there.

According to Gladys, her father drank like a fish and he came home most nights roaring drunk and incapable. I used to think he couldn't have been so incapable otherwise her mother couldn't have had nineteen children, could she?

Gladys wasn't a pretty girl by any means, neither was I, but she had a very lively personality and she certainly knew how to look after herself. Coming from a place like Stepney I suppose she had to, with all those brothers and sisters and a father who drank. She'd learnt how to take the buffets of life and still come up smiling. No one could put much over on Gladys. She used to give me a lot of good advice. One of the things she told me, she said, 'Never, never at any time when you meet a boyfriend, let on that you're in domestic service, because if you do you'll only be called a skivvy and you'll never keep him.' So I said, 'What shall I say I do then?' 'Oh tell them any old yarn, tell them you work in a shop or in a factory.' I said, 'Well, factory girls aren't any better than us.' 'They are in a boyfriend's eyes,' she said. 'Anyone that works in domestic service is a skivvy and they never bother about them. The very fact that our hours are limited is enough to put anyone off for a start.' I followed all this instruction but I really couldn't see it mattered much because the only young men that we ever met were the Red Coats from the Knightsbridge Barracks, the soldiers.

They never had any spare cash at all, or if they had, none of them ever spent a penny on us. All we ever did was wander round the park for hours on end or listen to the soapbox orators at Marble Arch. We had to be in at ten o'clock sharp, so the goodbyes weren't prolonged. A lot of inane remarks from the men and a lot of giggles from us, a few kisses and further promises to be sure to meet them at the same time next week, but neither Gladys nor I had any intention of having permanent dates with such ill-paid escorts.

It wasn't our idea of romance to walk around Hyde Park for hours on end with a couple of Red Coats and never get anything out of them.

Gladys and I were avid readers of those women's magazines of the time; things like *Peg's Paper*, *The Red Circle Magazine*, and the *Red Heart*. Between their pages many a poor and lonely heroine ended up marrying some Rudolph Valentino sort of man, or a Rothschild with loads of money. Of course the girl, in spite of her upbringing, always had a lovely almond-shaped face and beautiful liquid violet eyes, and although Gladys and I hadn't got these attributes, it didn't prevent us from dreaming that we had and that one day our prince would come. My idea of heaven at that time was a place where there was absolutely no work to do.

Gladys had a very vivid imagination, maybe Stepney is a place where vivid imagination is the only thing that keeps you going. She used to be able to rattle off details of an imaginary job to any boyfriends that she got to know. It was useless for me to pretend that I did any other sort of work except physical work because my hands were always so red and raw, and that was a dead give-away. How could they be anything else because there weren't rubber gloves in those days, or if there were kitchen maids didn't wear them, and barrier-cream certainly hadn't been invented. Even if it had, by the time I'd done the front stone steps and the brass in the morning and all the washing-up that followed done in strong soda water, it wouldn't have made any difference.

I think one of the things I hated most was doing the steps with hearthstone. Nowadays if you do hearthstone your steps, and not many people do, you can buy it in a packet of powder, but we used to have a big lump like a beach stone, and had to rub it hard on the steps. There you were in a sacking apron with your bottom sticking out and the errand boys throwing cheeky remarks at you. In the beginning I tried to do the steps from the bottom one up, but I couldn't because I tipped forward. They had to be done from the top down.

Another pet hate was cleaning the copper saucepans. Every time they were used they got filthy. All the bright polish would be tarnished after every meal. They had to be cleaned with a horrible mixture of silver sand, salt, vinegar, and a little flour. You mixed all this into a paste and then rubbed it on with your bare hands. You couldn't put it on with rags because you couldn't get the pressure that way, you dug your hand into the tin where you had previously mixed it all up and you rubbed it on the copper outside. It was a foul job. Every morning I had to do it. Mind you they looked lovely when I'd done them, they used to hang all along the wall in the kitchen, right from the very tiniest little saucepan, which didn't hold more than a teacup full, to the most enormous one in which you could put three Christmas puddings side by side. And there was a big fish-kettle as well. I used to get so miserable sometimes that I used to wish that they'd all get ptomaine poisoning from them. I was always being told that if I didn't clean them properly they'd get ptomaine poisoning. If they had they might have changed their saucepans.

They did eventually change them I heard afterwards

because the new kitchen maid flatly refused to clean them. I often wonder what would have happened if I'd refused to. I suppose they'd just have given me a month's notice.

After I'd been there a year I did give in my notice, and a very nerve-racking procedure that was. First, of course, I had to tell Mrs Bowchard, the cook, and that brought on, as I knew it would, a long diatribe on the ingratitude of young people in general and kitchen maids in particular. 'You train them,' she moaned, 'and for what? As soon as they've picked your brains they go off somewhere else.' She continued in this strain for some moments, glaring at me all the time.

It was a lot of tripe. She never taught me how to do any of her special dishes, the things I really wanted to know. All the ordinary stuff you can pick up out of a book, but every good cook has specialities with that little something that's not in any cookery book. Many a time I'd ask her what made a particular thing taste like this or how it turned out like that, but she would never tell me, 'that's the cook's secret', she would say. It was most unfair because when you go as kitchen maid you've taken the worst job in the house, you work harder than anyone else and you wait on servants because you eventually hope to have the best job in the house, the cook's. So it really is up to the cook, if you are doing a good job for her, to return it by helping you.

Anyway, my notice. I got over the ordeal of telling her. The next thing of course was to see Madam. I really don't think there was much to choose between them, they were both terrifying ogres as far as I was concerned. But the performance when you want to see Madam and you are only a kitchen maid! First you've got to ask the parlourmaid to ask Madam if she could spare you a few minutes of her time, and you have to say it in the tone of voice that shows you know Madam's time is so very precious.

During the year that I'd worked there I don't think that I'd seen Madam more than a dozen times, because when Mrs Bowchard knew that she was coming down to the kitchen, if I looked particularly scruffy which of course I often did, she'd just shoo me out until Madam had gone. No one considered that the reason why the kitchen looked so clean, the table white as snow, and the copper saucepans as burnished gold, was the reason you were so scruffy. So, as I say, I really only saw Madam about a dozen times and even then I don't think she saw me. She didn't appear to because she looked right through me.

Anyway, through the parlourmaid Madam graciously gave me an audience at ten o'clock the next morning and I gave her a month's notice. She naturally wanted to know the reason, 'Aren't you happy here?', with the slightly indignant air that meant how could anyone work in her house and not be happy? And, 'You wouldn't find a better place anywhere', and she was sure I must have learnt a lot. I said that the work was too hard and the hours were too long. Well, much to my astonishment she said she'd get help for me, that if would stay on she would get an odd-job man to help out. I would still have preferred to leave, but I was so overcome anyone really wanting me that I couldn't get over it. I found myself agreeing to stay, and I even said that I liked the job.

I must have been stark raving mad. But you see no one

had ever wanted me to stay before except one boyfriend, and I knew what he wanted me to stay for.

Even Mrs Bowchard, that old harridan of a cook, looked slightly less grim when I told her that Madam had asked me to stay on. She said, 'Is she giving you more money?' I'll bet if I'd said yes she'd have been up there herself the following day. So I said, 'No, she isn't giving me any more money but I'm going to have an odd-job man to help out.' Of course, she had to say, 'Girls aren't what they used to be in my days, you all want pampering now. But never mind,' she went on, 'it's better than having to train another girl. I'd sooner you stayed than have to start all over again. When you've had one kitchen maid you've had them all.' On she went. I'd heard it all before. I didn't take any notice.

Anyway, every morning except Sunday we used to have a man called Old Tom. I don't know if he had a surname, we only knew him as Old Tom. He used to come in at six o'clock and he worked for an hour and a half, and I can't tell you what bliss it was not to have to go out and do those front steps. It didn't matter Old Tom doing them. Nobody throws ribald remarks at a man scrubbing with his rear sticking up to high heaven. He used to do the boots and shoes, and get all the coal in as well, it was absolute heaven. I stayed there another year after that, I didn't find it nearly so hard. It was too good to be true.

# 18

EVERYTHING NOW went on very much the same in the house – the same routine broken by dinner parties and 'at homes'.

The 'at homes' didn't really affect me, not workwise, but they interested me. Everybody used to have them once a month – Mrs Cutler's used to be on the first Thursday, and there'd be a constant procession from half past three to about five. Mostly women, but a few gentlemen – they'd just come in, say, 'How do you do?', have a cup of tea, and rush off again, presumably to someone else's 'at home'. 'Keeping in the swim' I suppose they called it.

In the swim! The parlourmaids I know would have liked to have pushed their heads under and drowned them. The parlourmaids had to do all the work; cutting platefuls of thin bread and butter and anointing them with some stuff called Gentlemen's Relish. I don't know if you can still get it, or why it was called that. I didn't like the nasty salty stuff. I suppose it gave gentlemen a thirst for the drinks they had at around half past five.

Madam was always on the look-out for new ideas for these 'at homes', and used to badger the cook and parlourmaids. Sort of putting one over on the Joneses. I suppose they still do it today at debs' dances – trying to get the latest beat band, and things like that.

But it didn't affect me like the dinner parties. Although it meant a lot of extra work and a bad-tempered Mrs Bowchard, there was always a sense of 'occasion' about these dinner parties. You could feel it in the kitchen, but you could see it upstairs.

I always used to try and pop up to the dining-room before dinner. The table would be laid out with a lace cloth that was a family heirloom, it was a wonderful thing, all handmade, and you can imagine the size it was to stretch out on to a dining-room table that had two more leaves put in it. It was the most marvellous one of its kind I've ever seen. In the centre was a crystal epergne, the silver was all Georgian. With that, and the two crystal chandeliers with the candles lit, it used to look like a scene from the Arabian nights.

I do think that when you had a cloth on, even if it wasn't a lace cloth but a snowy white damask, it looked a lot better than all these bits and dabs of mats do today, stuck all over the table.

Mrs Bowchard was never the soul of amiability, but on a dinner party day she was something too terrible for words. A sort of aura of grimness and unapproachability enveloped her. You would have thought she was cooking for Buckingham Palace and a regiment of Guards all at once. It used to make the work that much harder. But the most exciting part about these dinner parties was the chauffeurs who used to bring the guests. They would stay and sit in our servants' hall while their employers were upstairs.

You never saw such a fluttering in the dovecote as there used to be on these occasions. There we were, six or seven of us women who hardly ever spoke to a man and whose femininity was so suppressed that we got to be like female eunuchs. We would suddenly realize that we'd got a sex, that we were real females. So noses would be powdered, hair all fripped up, and waists pulled in. People had waists in those days, there were none of these shifts. Bosoms were stuck out, and rears stuck out, so if you pulled the waist in, you looked like an hourglass, but it was fashionable then. Even Flora, the head parlourmaid, and Annie, the head housemaid, both well over forty and resigned to a life of spinsterhood, would become one of the girls for the night. Our servants' hall would be a sort of magnet for the females, even the sewing-maid and the nursemaid would find some excuse or other to come down. And all because of these chauffeurs in their uniforms.

Probably they were the most nondescript collection of men in private life. It's like the soldiers in the war, isn't it? They all looked so handsome when they were wandering around in uniform, but if you met them in civvies you wouldn't cross the road to speak to them, well half of them anyway, especially the American ones.

To Gladys and me these chauffeurs looked simply wonderful, and to be actually able to speak to these hundred-percent men in leggings was something too glorious for words.

It's a sad fact that uniform does nothing for a woman at

all, it just accentuates all the wrong bulges, but even the most insignificant male seems to look masculine when he's got a uniform on. Maybe because it's cut to show off whatever points he has got (I'm not being vulgar), I mean to accentuate them.

They were, of course, delighted to be the centre of interest. What man wouldn't be if he had five or six females fluttering around him, plying him with biscuits, and cups of tea, and hanging on to his words with bated breath. Men are very susceptible to flattery. Even a man with a face like the back of a bus, if you tell him he doesn't look too bad, believes you. You can stuff men up with any old yarn. They believe anything. You've only got to gaze into their eyes, and sound as though you mean what you say. I've tried it so I know it's true.

They used to tell scandalous stories about the gentry. Anybody upstairs was called the gentry in those days. We would hear all about their employers. The good, the bad, the spicy. They used to talk about their affairs. A lot of the male gentry had what was known in those days as a love nest, a flat they'd set up for some woman, and the chauffeurs used to drive them to it. That was really the extent of their knowledge. They never went into the flat, they never actually knew what went on. But to listen to them you would have thought that they'd partaken of the love feast. Using the royal 'we' like Mrs Bowchard's brother-in-law, they would take us through the whole ceremony in all its amorous detail. They couldn't have known it but, I suppose, it wasn't hard to surmise.

In any case some of them were chauffeur/valets and I've no doubt were looked upon as a sort of respository of secrets by their employers. They knew that they were never likely to talk on social terms to anyone that mattered, and it probably got it off their conscience if they had one. Anyway, men like to talk about that sort of thing.

I used to work for a man myself who had a little place on the seafront. And when the rest of the family were in London he often used to pop down and go round to this little love nest.

People used to expect it of men. Mind you, if it was a woman doing it . . . Now there's the unfairness of life, you couldn't set up a love nest for a man, and yet maybe you would like to. It's like those 'red light' districts, isn't it? Why should men have the advantages in their sexual life? When all's said and done women can have husbands who don't supply enough, and I think there should be places where they can go where all the men have been vetted and are ready to oblige for a small fee. We are the underprivileged sex, really and truly, in every way of life.

But to come back to the chauffeurs – it may seem a nasty kind of conversation for them to have had, but it was the same with all the upper servants. Their own lives were so devoid of excitement that they had to find all their life vicariously. Sexual life, social life, every sort of life.

Employers constantly, by the things they talked about in front of servants, left themselves open to blackmail. But we would never have known how to set about it. That sort of thing has come with more education, with the greater freedom of the press. We had the feeling that what they upstairs did, although it was a subject of scandal and gossip and laughter, was their privilege. Not because they were better than us, but because they had money and it was no good having money if you couldn't deviate from the norm.

It was shortly after I had agreed to stay on with Mrs Cutler that something happened which still stands out in my mind like a scene from a Victorian melodrama. It was discovered that Agnes, the under-parlourmaid, was going to have a baby.

Nowadays it's all so vastly different; so much do they want you now in domestic service that I'm sure that if your employers found you were going to have a baby they'd say,'Yes, well bad luck. But you'll be sure and come back when you've had it, won't you?' You see them advertising, saying one child not objected to. They're as good as saying all right, you've got an illegitimate baby, we're quite prepared to accept the child as well.

In those days it was slam the door, dismissal with no money, your own home probably closed to you, nothing left but the streets or the workhouse.

Gladys and I shared a bedroom with Agnes and although I'd seen her being sick as soon as she got out of bed, I didn't realize that it was one of the symptoms of having a baby. I just thought she had sudden bilious attacks. It did seem strange that as soon as she got on her feet it happened, and that she was all right during the day, but that's what I put it down to.

Eventually Gladys, who was far more versed in all these

things than I was, asked her outright if she was pregnant. It sounded a terrible word that 'pregnant'. Agnes admitted that she was and implored us to keep it a secret. It hadn't gone very long and it didn't show yet.

But clothes in those days weren't designed to conceal your tummy. You had a waistline with a belt and it was very difficult indeed. I wished with all my heart that I could help Agnes but I hadn't the faintest idea what to do. It was Gladys who knew a bit, and she did try.

She bought bottles of pennyroyal pills which were supposed to be very good at getting rid of it, Beecham's pills, and quinine. But all they did for Agnes was to make her spend half the day in the lavatory. Then on Gladys' instructions we used to lug hot water up the stairs to fill the hip bath for her. Then we'd tip tins of mustard in it, until it was absolutely yellow. That was supposed to be another good thing, hot mustard baths. Maybe it would have been if Agnes could have got her waist in it, but she couldn't. Then she tried carrying all the heavy weights she could, and when it was her day off she used to go in the park, climb on to the park benches and then keep jumping off. It sounds amusing, but it was a terrible thing for her. She tried shifting furniture. She would pick up a massive armchair, they were huge in those days, and move it from one part of the room to the other. But none of it did any good.

Eventually, of course, she couldn't hide it from Mrs Cutler, and poor Agnes was told to leave at the end of week.

It's impossible nowadays to imagine what it must have been like for her. Although Gladys and I were terribly sorry

about it, it was like when you go into hospital and somebody's dying of something, you've got that faint feeling of
rejoicing that it isn't you, and Gladys and I both felt that;
above our sympathy we were thankful it wasn't us that were
in this predicament.

Although Madam told her to leave at the end of the week
she did give her a month's wages. But the very fact that she
did this convinced me in my suspicions as to who the father
was. Agnes would never tell. I didn't expect her to tell
Madam, but she wouldn't tell Gladys and me who it was, and
I knew she knew, because she wasn't the sort of girl that
would have gone with any Tom, Dick, and Harry; it just had
to be one man and one man alone. I suspected it was a nephew
of Mrs Cutler's. He was very young, probably in his early
twenties, and a very handsome man. He had such an attractive voice that even to hear him say good morning used to
make you feel frivolous. It sent shivers all up and down you.
I suspected him because on several occasions I discovered
him on the back staircase, which was our staircase, a place
where he certainly had no right to be at all. He used to say
good morning or good afternoon to me in this marvellous,
attractive voice of his. Some of the Americans have voices
like that I have since discovered.

I think Mrs Cutler was worried, because I think she knew,
or she was nearly certain it was this nephew. She questioned
Gladys and me closely and though we said we didn't know,
she didn't believe us.

Even though she thought it was her own flesh and blood
that was responsible I had to listen to such a long lecture on

the evils of such wanton behaviour. No nice young man would ever suggest such a thing to a girl he hoped to marry. Have you ever heard such drivel because that's one of the things they always suggested. Whether they're likely to marry you or not, they like to try their goods out first. I've never been out with a man that didn't suggest it, believe me. And Mrs Cutler went on that no decent girl would ever let a man take advantage of her.

Well now, that's another ridiculous remark, because the ratio of girls to young men was so high that if you had a young man and you cared about him and he suggested this, it seemed to be the only way to keep him. You had a hard job not to do it if you were not going to be stuck without a young man at all, and if you were dying to get out of domestic service, which most of us were. What did Mrs Cutler know about human nature in the basement? The only thing that kept me and those like me from straying off the straight and narrow was ignorance and fear. Ignorance of how not to have a baby, and fear of catching a disease. We were always told that you only had to go with a young man and you'd catch venereal disease. That's why so many deviate now because those two fears have gone, haven't they? The disease can be cured, and the baby can be taken care of, even if you have it. Now they encourage you to get rid of it before it gets to anything.

But Agnes wasn't like Gladys or me; Gladys came from an enormous family, had a very hard life, and was a realist; I was just frightened of what might happen. And ignorant. I did know roughly what you had to do to have a baby, but I didn't know what you could do and *not* have one. But Agnes was a soft girl, very sentimental, starry-eyed, and when she went to the films she would come back with all dreams and things.

I remember she used to have a crush on Cesar Romero. Gladys and I got turned out of the cinema when we went to see Cesar Romero because I said to Gladys, 'Hasn't he got lovely teeth?' and she said, 'Yes, and I bet he's got another set at home.' And we laughed so much they made us leave. But to poor Agnes, Cesar Romero was a god.

So you can imagine if it was Mrs Cutler's nephew with that marvellous voice of his, he would know how to treat a girl, and make her feel she was really something, not just an under-parlourmaid with no money and no position. And Agnes was a pretty girl too, and her prettiness was natural, she never used any artificial aids. I can quite see how she was overcome. And he bought her presents, I know because she had some silk underwear. She said it came from her home, but I don't think it could have.

All right, it may not have been him, but I have a very strong suspicion that it was, and Mrs Cutler did too. Anyway what was he doing on our back stairs? They didn't lead anywhere except to the maids' bedrooms.

But going back to ignorance, fear, and straying off the straight and narrow, the whole idea of lovemaking was tied up with the idea it was sinful and revolting. Even the married relationship was often ruined because of this way of thinking.

I remember about a year after I was married I chanced to meet a girl I'd known in service and we went into a tea shop to talk about old times. She told me she'd been married for five years, and when I made an inquiry into whether she had any family she burst out, 'Oh, I hate all that side of married life. I can't bear George even to kiss me because I know he's leading up to "that".' She would never put it into words, it was 'that'. Well, I remarked that her mother couldn't have felt like that, she'd had twelve children, the mother had. She said, 'Oh, it was my Dad, he'd never leave her alone. Even when she was hanging the washing on the line he would creep up behind her, and in the daylight too!' I was thrown half-mast at this! Laugh? Her 'in the daylight too', it sounded so funny. And when I said to her, 'Well, it was a blessed interlude on a wash day,' she was so incensed that she stalked out and I had to finish my tea on my own. But I couldn't help bursting out, could I? It was a pleasant interlude.

Although much of what I have said may make you think I was envious of the lives of other people this wasn't really the case. It was the inequality and the unfairness that struck me so much of the time. But there was one person of whom I was both jealous and envious: Miss Susan, the eldest of Mrs Cutler's grandchildren. She was only two years younger than I was, but what a different life hers was from mine! She was almost as tall as I was, and she had the same sort of hair colouring, but there the resemblance finished completely, because Miss Susan was and had everything that I wasn't and hadn't. She had masses of clothes, a horse to ride, a tennis court to play on. She could speak French, play the piano, sing well; I was envious of her life, envious of all her accomplishments. Not all the time. But when she came down into the kitchen to ask for something and I was at the sink, you know, immersed in bowls of greasy water, washing saucepans, my hair straight as pump water, clad in a sacking apron, and there she was, only two years younger than me, tripping in, dressed up to the nines, and with her cultivated voice asking for something which I would immediately have to rush to get for her, I wouldn't have been human if I hadn't felt envious. Everything was done for her, the under-nurse used to brush her hair, her bath was got ready, even the toothpaste used to be laid on the brush ready for her.

Sometimes she came with a message for the cook, and Mrs Bowchard would be all smiles for Miss Susan. It would be, 'Oh yes, Miss Susan', 'No, Miss Susan', 'Certainly, Miss Susan'. And when she had gone Mrs Bowchard would say to me, 'Doesn't she look a picture, she's a sight for sore eyes, a ray of sunshine.' It seemed to hurt. Once I had the temerity to say, 'If only she'd had to work down here for a week she wouldn't be such a ray of sunshine.' Mrs Bowchard, she was furious with me. She said, 'You're just eaten up with jealousy because you could never hope to look like that, even if you had money you couldn't look or behave like Miss Susan.' I don't think I really begrudged Miss Susan her place in life, it was just the contrast was so marked when she came into our kitchen. And you see she never spoke to me or even noticed me. You would have thought she would have done. I was another young girl of about her own age. So I thought she was stuck up, but it could have been she was being tactful, that she noticed the contrast between what I was and what she was, so I might have been doing her an injustice now that I look back on it.

# 19

CHRISTMAS IN domestic service was nothing like the Christmases we had at home. I remember the excitement there was at home even with little money, the excitement of waking up early, the rush into our parents' room for the presents and stockings. We didn't have turkeys or Christmas trees, but we had plenty of laughter and there was always enough food to eat.

Christmas in Mrs Cutler's house was a very formal and elaborate affairs. There used to be a large tree in the dining-room which was decorated by the nanny.

On Christmas Day after breakfast all the servants had to line up in the hall. Being the lowest in status I was at the end of the line. Then we had to file into the dining-room where all the family, Mr and Mrs Cutler, and the daughter, and the grandchildren, were assembled complete with Christmas smiles, and social-welfare expressions. The children looked at us as though we were beings from another world. And I suppose to them we were really sub-beings from a sub-world.

It used to remind me of those adverts with blacks all walking along. I used to keep kidding Gladys, trying to make her laugh. But you couldn't really laugh, it was such a solemn occasion. Talk about Christmas! When we got to the Christmas tree we deferentially accepted the parcels that were handed to us by the children, and muttered, 'Thank you, Master Charles, thank you, Miss Susan.' Oh I hated it all.

Then we had to go to the Master and Madam and were given an envelope containing money; I used to have a pound and Mrs Bowchard had five pounds. The presents were always something useful; print dress lengths, aprons, black stockings, not silk, of course, they never gave you anything frivolous; black woollen stockings. How I longed for some of the things they had, silk underwear, perfume, jewellery, why couldn't they have given us something like that? Why did we always have to have sensible things? I think that the reason they used to give us uniforms was because they knew we couldn't buy them out of our measly wages. Besides if we were to have perfume or silk we would go astray. So I hated this parade of Christmas goodwill, and the pretence that we also had a good time at Christmas.

We had to work like trojans, coping with their dinner parties and the other entertaining that went on upstairs. All right, we had a Christmas tree in our servants' hall that they'd bought, but they never put anything on it; we had to decorate it up with tinsel and bells and things, and they didn't put their presents on it. We had to line up before them in Indian file accepting their alms. That was Christmas there.

It was a replica of all the Christmases I had in domestic

service. Formal and elaborate, a lot of entertaining by them, but nothing much for us. I dare say in the very large establishments they would arrange a servants' ball like they do at Buckingham Palace. But from what I know of that sort of thing it never took place at Christmas, it was always well afterwards.

About two months after Christmas we had to start on the spring-cleaning. That was a major operation, and lasted for four weeks. Spring-cleaning in those days was done with nothing, I mean no Hoovers, no mechanical aids, no modern detergents, nothing. People don't spring-clean nowadays, they just keep their houses clean all the year round.

During these four weeks I got up at five o'clock every morning and I worked until about eight o'clock at night. Then I had to get supper for the servants after that. We all worked these hours, but, of course, I remember mine in particular because it was mine that made me tired, not theirs! I used to crawl up to bed, too weary even to wash. I know it sounds dirty, but you work from five till eight doing spring cleaning in an old-fashioned house where they have coal fires in every room, and you'd be very weary.

The first job was to scrub all the stone floors in the basement using a mixture of soap and sand. Those stone floors in the basement weren't like those very shiny tiles that you see in front porches or kitchens nowadays. They were pitted and those pittings used to get filled with dirt, and only a mixture of soap and sand and a scrubbing-brush would get it out. All the iron and copper saucepans had to be cleaned on the outside even more than usual, and the huge steel fender and fire had to be polished until it looked like new, every bit of china had to be washed (there was enough to stock a shop), and the long kitchen tables, and the chairs and the dresser all had to be scrubbed until they were white. My hands used to get raw and bleeding and my nails broken and jagged.

Upstairs it was easier for the house- and parlourmaids, there wasn't so much scrubbing. The carpets were the worst things there. In those days people had hundreds of little china ornaments all of which had to be washed.

Spring-cleaning the silver was a major operation. In this particular house, and in the majority like it, the silver was stored in a safe and the working silver was put in it every night. The safe was a sort of room that led off the dining-room, its door concealed by a screen. You could walk right into it. There were tea sets, not just one, a number, coffee sets, candelabras, table centres, and silver salvers; it used to look like an Aladdin's Cave. They used jeweller's rouge, not one of these white pastes in tins that are used nowadays, then polish with a leather and a brush. It was a long operation to make sure that none of the stuff was ever left in the little cracks and crevices.

Although we had to work these long hours we didn't get any extra money. But as a treat for this particular job Mrs Cutler used to book us seats at the theatre. Half of the staff went one week, and half the next. I remember the last show I went to, it was a comedy. But I didn't really enjoy it because we were in the expensive seats, sitting among the well-to-do, and I felt conspicuous wearing a somewhat shabby black coat and a pair of black cotton gloves which I didn't dare take off because my hands were all red and raw. I remember the following morning the cook said to me, 'Did you have a good time?' I said, 'Oh it was all right.' So she said, 'Well, don't forget to say thank you tomorrow morning to Madam for the evening out that she gave you.' So I replied with great boldness, 'Well, Madam hasn't said thank you to me for all the extra work I've done for her.' I thought the cook would have suffocated with rage. 'You're here to work,' she said, 'and if you don't like the job we can very soon get another kitchen maid.'

Anyway, by this time I'd been a kitchen maid nearly three years, and after three years of being the lowest, and the lowliest-paid servant, I reckoned I could get by as a trained cook. At least I knew how to cook vegetables, make sauces and I thought I'd learnt a few other things as I'd gone along.

So I looked in the papers and at last I saw an advertisement . . . Good plain cook wanted; it was for a house in Kensington. So I wrote. I had to put two years on to my age because I thought if I told them how old I was they wouldn't employ me. I was sure they would consider eighteen too young to be a cook. I got a reply and was asked to go for an interview.

On the appointed day I presented myself at the house, not without some trepidation, because it's a tremendous jump from kitchen maid to cook. When I got there the usual inquisition followed. Madam started off with, 'How old are you?' 'Twenty,' I lied. 'Is your home in London? Are you afraid of work?'

Now of all the ridiculous questions to ask anyone, 'Are

you afraid of work?' There's a good many people who're not afraid of work who don't like it. If she'd have said, 'Do you like work?' it would have been just as silly. My idea of heaven at that time was a place where you didn't have anything to do except sit around fiddling with your harp.

This lady had a title, she was Lady Gibbons. But I could tell straight away she wasn't of the gentry. She told me there were three in the family; herself, Sir Walter Gibbons, and a son. 'How much money were you thinking of?' she asked. I heard a voice that didn't sound like mine saying, 'Forty pounds.' 'Forty pounds!' she echoed, as if I'd asked for the Crown Jewels. Then there was a pause as if she thought I'd reconsider it. I didn't. 'Yes,' I said, 'and I want one whole day off a month.' Her face fell still further. 'If I give you a whole day off every month,' she said, 'the housemaid and the parlourmaid will want one too.' I said nothing. Just sat silent.

I've always found it's the best defence, be quiet, don't answer, then they felt that although you disagreed with them you realized it wasn't your place to argue with your betters. This attitude usually paid off. In any case although servants were still two-a-penny, the first rumblings of revolt at wages and conditions were beginning to be heard, and it wasn't so easy to give next to nothing and hardly any time off.

I got the job. Forty pounds a year and my day off a month as well.

Once again I had the unpleasant task of giving a month's notice to Mrs Cutler. This time there could be no inducements and she wouldn't offer me more money because once you give one servant any more money, everyone would ask for more. Once again I went through the ritual of making an appointment to see her as though she was some royalty. I laid on the old smarm and she laid on a little lecture. It could have been a lot worse.

The unpleasantness came from Mrs Bowchard. It wasn't that she had any personal animosity against me, she just didn't like kitchen maids, she didn't really like anyone that was that much younger than herself. For a whole month I was subjected to a barrage of innuendoes about my capabilities as a cook. She'd say, 'Suppose they ask you to make so and so, how would you do it?' I didn't know how to do it, because I hadn't had a chance of learning, and I'd say, 'I'll get it out of a book.' 'Meg,' she'd say, 'you can't cook from a book, you learn from practical experience.' I'd say, 'But you've got to start.' 'I didn't start when I was eighteen, I was twenty-five before I thought I was anywhere near good enough,' she'd sneer. 'Times are changing, aren't they?' I'd reply. 'For the worse for Lady Gibbons. You only know how to do vegetables.' And then she'd start on about their digestions, how she hoped they'd got good ones; digging at me all the time.

Then of course I had to leave everything spotless so that when the new kitchen maid came it would all look marvellous. I knew just how Mrs Bowchard would be. When she got the new kitchen maid I would be praised, 'Ah, when I had Margaret, she was a good girl, she used to do this, that, and the other.' The last fortnight was the worst of the lot, but knowing I was going I didn't worry. I stayed as pleasant as I knew how to be.

The only one I was sorry to leave was Gladys. We'd got on

like a 'house on fire'; she'd come from a home as poor as mine, and she never built castles in the air. We'd just got on fine. One thing I did vow to myself was that if ever I was good enough a cook to have a kitchen maid I'd never be as foul to her as Mrs Bowchard had been to me.

# 20

I ARRIVED AT Lady Gibbons' full of confidence if not much
knowledge.

I got my first shock when I went to the servants' hall.
There I found the housemaid, Jessica, but no parlourmaid.
Jessica told me that there was a constant procession of housemaids and parlourmaids; nobody would stay long because of
Lady Gibbons' temper. 'She's an absolute cow,' Jessica said.
'Mean as a muck-worm, eyes like a gimlet, and a nose like a
bloodhound.' I thought, well this is fine, this is a lovely job
I've come into. I said, 'What do you mean, a nose like a bloodhound?' She said, 'If you use the gas stove because you've let
the fire get low, you'll find her at the top of the kitchen stairs
bawling down, "Are you using the gas stove, cook?" She can
smell it. That's what I mean.'

The following day I came to realize how parsimonious
Lady Gibbons was. I'd come from a house where the cook just
telephoned for everything she wanted. Where vast quantities
of milk and cream, eggs, and butter were used every day;

where caviare and pâté de foie gras were quite commonplace, and where any left-overs would be thrown in the pig bucket.

That first morning Lady Gibbons came into the kitchen, she walked into the larder and inspected every bit of food there. I'd never seen anything like that happen before, nor since. She peered into the old bread crock, she even counted the crusts. She looked into the flour bin and the vegetable rack and the ice box, and she ended up by counting the eggs. I was absolutely dumbfounded. I kept on imagining Mrs Bowchard's face if Mrs Cutler had come down and done the same thing. She wouldn't have stayed five minutes, she would have given her notice there and then.

My next shock was when she told me that she did all the ordering and that anything I wanted I'd have to ask for. She had a store cupboard in the basement and everything was all doled out to me in minute quantities, and the cupboard was then locked. I was never given the key.

For instance, the jam was ladled out of one of those big seven-pound jars as though it was so much gold dust. And the same with tea and other things – just enough for each day. Mind you, perhaps in some ways this was an advantage, inasmuch as I was very inexperienced and I wouldn't have known what to order, and running the store cupboard would just have been an added worry.

I think I should explain that when you go to a house as a 'good plain cook' you don't get a kitchen maid. Nor was there the large staff that I'd known before. There was just me, a chauffeur, a housemaid, and parlourmaid, and as I've said, often only one of the last two.

When it came to what to call me, Lady Gibbons was in a quandary. The two other cooks I'd known had been called 'Mrs' even though they weren't married; a sort of courtesy title, but Lady Gibbons said I was too young to be called 'Mrs'. She called the other servants by their surnames, but I didn't like that, so we settled for 'cook'.

She wanted me to wear a cap, but I wouldn't. It always struck me as a badge of servitude. I know nurses wear caps but somehow it's different with them. In any case it was a hideous cap, so I left it off. Lady Gibbons didn't like it, but she couldn't really do anything about it.

During the morning the parlourmaid used to have to go upstairs to help the housemaid make the beds. And while she was upstairs Lady Gibbons asked me if I would answer the front door. I used to wear print dresses with short sleeves that finished at my elbow; one morning she came down with a cap and a pair of white cotton armlets that fitted from the wrist up to the elbow, and she said, 'Oh, I've brought you these down, cook, because I think you would feel more comfortable if you went to the front door wearing them.' She didn't think I would feel more comfortable at all, what she really meant was that *she* would feel a lot more comfortable. So I said, 'Oh yes, thank you, M'Lady,' because you used to have to say 'M'Lady'; naturally, being a titled Lady, you didn't say Madam. 'Yes thank you, M'Lady.' And I just put them away in my drawer. I never did put them on. She never said anything more. She knew the rules; they were not written down but they were all there unwritten. She knew that she could no more compel me to wear a cap and those armlets than fly.

When I started cooking I found out that it was quite true what Mrs Bowchard had said, that there was more to it than following the books, more to it even than experience; you had to have a kind of instinct about it, and I didn't seem to have much in the way of instinct at that time.

One dish I came a cropper on was beef-olives. I'd watched Mrs Bowchard make these, she used to use the best fillet steak, cut it into thin slices, and then put a little veal force-meat on each slice, roll it up, tie it with very thin twine, and cook it in a casserole. When you've cooked them you cut the twine off and serve them up. It's a dish which is full of flavour. Lady Gibbons was very fond of salt beef, and would have it as a hot dish on a Sunday perhaps, served with carrots and boiled onions. It was very economical. When it was cold she used to want me to make beef-olives with it. Well, when you cut and fold a slice of cold salt beef, it cracks everywhere. I used to tie them up in little bundles, putting string this way and that. Then of course when they were cooked I couldn't get the string off, it had embedded itself in. So I sent them up as they were. When the three plates came down all the bits of string were round the edge in a sort of silent reproach.

This sort of thing didn't dampen my spirits. I was as lively as a cricket at that time. It's a funny thing, but the less cooking you know how to do, the more competent you feel. It's only when you know how to cook that it worries you when it goes wrong, because when you don't know, you don't know it's gone wrong. The more experienced I got the more I worried. I soon realized when a dish wasn't perfection. Not that I could have hoped to have a dish that was perfection at

Lady Gibbons' because even the best cook in the world can't make a dish out of poor ingredients.

The reason I was so cheerful was because of my metamorphosis of kitchen maid to cook. The difference in status can only be understood by somebody who's been in domestic service. As a kitchen maid you're a nobody, a nothing, you're not listened to, you're even a skivvy to the other servants. All right, as a cook with only two other servants you're not looked upon as God Almighty, but I didn't want that. I didn't want to be better than everybody else, I just wanted not to have somebody continually carping all the time at me.

Although Lady Gibbons was an old cow, I usually only saw her in the mornings when she came down to give orders. She used to moan about some of the things I did. After I'd been there a week, for instance, she came down and looked at the kitchen table and she said to me, 'Cook,' she said, 'this table's getting awfully yellow.' I said, 'Is it? Must be the colour of the wood, M'Lady.' So she said, 'Well, it must have changed its colour since you came here then.' But it didn't dampen my spirits.

After I'd been there a few weeks, Jessica the housemaid left. The new parlourmaid, Olive, was only fifteen years old. A parlourmaid only fifteen years old, even under-parlourmaids are often older than that! Lady Gibbons generally got very young girls as housemaids or parlourmaids and what she called 'trained' them. She did this because she got them very much cheaper, and also because she was getting so well known among the fraternity of domestic servants that she couldn't get anybody that was experienced.

Olive was a country girl. She came from a remote little village three miles from a railway station or a bus. She was exceptionally good-looking with beautiful eyes, lovely black hair, and with a most placid disposition. She needed it at Lady Gibbons'. She became a life-long friend of mine.

Sir Walter was a quiet man, he seemed to be sunk in reveries of past glories, and was oblivious to what went on around him. He'd been somebody abroad. I don't quite know what. With the East India Company perhaps; he certainly had a brown complexion. Lady Gibbons would sometimes expound about Sir Walter, 'When Sir Walter dined with the Maharajah . . .', so I got the impression that he had been somebody at one time.

And I also got the impression that his marriage to Lady Gibbons had been his greatest mistake and had dragged him down socially. She spoke like a fishwife and seemed to have had no kind of education at all. Talk about Gibbon's 'Decline and Fall', she was it.

He only ever came to life at meal times. I remember Olive reporting to me that he had commented that good cooks were a dying race so he had a sense of humour. Looking back he needed it with some of the dishes I served. I remember another occasion. In that house the food lift was situated in the kitchen, and when pulled up went through the dining-room floor, thus noises in the kitchen could be heard. I'd been singing merrily all the evening as I sent up each course, and Sir Walter evidently couldn't stand any more of it because he came to the lift and called down, 'Cook, will you sing "God Save the King" and finish the concert?'

But Lady Gibbons used to impress all of us with the importance of her title. She used to say, 'When you speak of me don't call me Lady Gibbons, say "Her Ladyship", and similarly when you're speaking to Sir Walter, don't say "Yes, Sir", say "Yes, Sir Walter, No, Sir Walter".' One day Olive came down with a water jug on a salver, and she walked round the table saying, 'Water, Sir Walter? Water, Sir Walter?' much to our amusement.

Although there were only three in the family the work wasn't all that easy. I still had to get up early to light the kitchen range; Sir Walter couldn't have his bath until that range had been on some time. Then I had to get an early breakfast for the son, about half past seven in the morning. He went to business. Then there was our breakfast at eight o'clock, and Sir Walter and Lady Gibbons' breakfast at nine. Then before she came down at ten to give the orders I had to scrub out the kitchen and the scullery, and tidy the servants' hall and the larder, because she used to look at everything.

The parlourmaid, poor Olive, had plenty to do, especially in the winter when the coal fires had to be lit. She had to carry scuttles of coal from the basement to the ground floor for the dining-room, and to the first floor for the drawing-room. And they had a fire in the breakfast room as well. These three fires had to be lit every morning by eight, and only half a bundle of wood was allowed for each. Some mornings poor Olive could do it on her head, but other mornings when the wind was in the wrong direction she just couldn't get them to go. She used to keep dashing up and down carrying cups of paraffin. And the tears ran down her face, mingling with the soot.

The housemaid was lucky, because they were so mean they never had fires in the bedrooms.

An odd thing happened there which I've never seen before or since. They used warming-pans. Now warming-pans really went out long before that time, but Lady Gibbons had two. One used to hang in the hall as an ornament, but into the other one we used to rake the hot coals from the range each night and run them over the beds. I used to think we were better off, because on winter nights I used to put bricks in the oven and we used to wrap them up in a bit of flannel and put them in our beds. Believe me, I am sure we used to have better benefit from those bricks than they did from their warming-pans.

There was only one attic room and Olive and I shared it. I could have had the room on the floor below, but I let the housemaid have that because I wanted to be as far away from 'Them' as I possibly could be. Lady Gibbons thought it was very unusual that the cook should share, because she always had a room of her own, and the housemaid and parlourmaid shared. But I preferred the attic.

At Lady Gibbons' I had every Sunday afternoon and one afternoon a week off, as well as the whole day once a month that I'd stipulated. Olive only got alternate Sundays. But when it was possible we used to go out on Sunday afternoon together to a tea-dance. They sound quite hectic affairs and would be today probably, but then they were very innocuous dos. You mostly went with a partner. If you went with a girl you might have to dance with her all afternoon.

But you went there of course in the hopes of picking up a

boyfriend. That was really the only opportunity you had of meeting one. If you went to watch a film, for instance, and a young man sat next to you and started nudging you and all that, you naturally thought the worst. Anyway, you could hardly see what he was like in the dark, and you couldn't very well converse. When anyone nudged me he usually turned out to have a face like Frankenstein's monster and morals of the farmyard, so I didn't dare chance it often. But at a tea-dance you could study the opposite sex and if there was anyone you fancied you could go all out to get them. And believe me when we went all out we went all out.

You see I was determined to get married. I didn't want to be an old maid. In those days people put on a very contemptuous expression when they talked about 'being on the shelf', or being a spinster. It meant you were lacking practically everything. Nowadays women who don't get married have often had all the sex they want and all the security. They just don't want to take a man for life, which I don't blame them for in the least. But I needed one to support me. I couldn't see myself being a cook for the rest of my time. I wanted one to take me on for life.

Olive, as well as being a good-looking girl, was an excellent dancer, far better than me, and as she was so attractive she always got plenty of partners. And the reason for her success was confidence.

She'd been brought up in a village and she'd always gone to the village dances. Parents used to take even their young children. So they learned early, and they had all the confidence in the world. I didn't really know how to dance at all.

I could never follow anyone. Being of a rather aggressive disposition, I was wanting to lug them around, instead of letting them take me around.

My only asset was that I could talk, and that's a doubtful asset on a dance floor. People don't go to dances for conversation, they go to dance and to see who they can collect to take home later. It really did me a disservice to be able to talk because I deviated from the norm in my conversation. It should go like this: the boy says to you, 'Do you come here often?' and you answer, 'Oh yes, fairly often,' then he says, 'Lovely floor, isn't it?' then you say, 'Oh yes, very springy.' Then he'd say, 'It's a good band, isn't it?' and you answer, 'Yes, it's got good rhythm, hasn't it?' Instead I'd talk to my partners about historical London, or ask them if they read Dickens. They must have thought I was some kind of freak. They'd never even heard of Dickens, let alone read any of him.

I was beginning to lap up culture; even in those days I always found time for reading, I mean books that were worth reading.

Sometimes I would try talking about Conrad, books a boy would like, Henty even, or O. Henry. But they'd never read anything like that at all, and I'd get dropped like a hot cake.

But Olive, she was a soulful, sentimental sort of girl, and would gaze up into their faces with a loving expression and have all the right answers at the right times. And she was a good dancer as well.

I've always found that when two girls go around together one of them's always more attractive than the other, and it was the same with Olive and me. She was much more attractive than I was. It's the same when you collect two boy-friends, there's one that's handsome and the other who's got a face like the back of a bus. I suppose it's nature's way of compensating.

Olive, although she'd come straight from the country and was only fifteen, used to collect boyfriends like bees round the proverbial honey pot. She knew how to talk to them too and keep them sort of dangling. There's an art in that sort of thing.

Naturally I got the dud one. Sometimes he wouldn't be too bad and I would think, well this is it. Another time it would be a receding chin, a vacuous kind of a creature, and I'd just stick him for one evening and then throw him up.

Although you may want to get married you've got to watch it. If you don't like a weak-chinned, vacuous kind of an individual for even a few hours, you're not going to want him sitting opposite you at the table every morning and every night of your life, are you? Olive used to say, 'You're too particular, what's it matter? Have him until you find another.' But how can you find another if you're going out with the same one all the time? 'Oh yes,' she said, 'you can.' She could. As I say there's an art in that kind of thing, I didn't get to know it, I never had the social graces. When I moaned about one, Olive used to say, 'Any port in a storm,' but it was never as stormy as that at the age of eighteen. Later on when I did get married I got a reasonably good-looking one.

Although Olive must have had endless opportunities, she didn't make the same mistake as Agnes. She seemed to have her head screwed on the right way. Again I put it down to village life.

Olive had been brought up in a Sussex village called Ripe. It sounds like a Cockney immoral assault. It wasn't the same as villages nowadays, with the young people trying to get away at the earliest opportunity. They had a social life, and the centre was the village hall.

People used to take their children to the various functions, thus from a very early age they mixed with the opposite sex. So it was that Olive never got as embarrassed with the opposite sex as I did. It's all very well to talk about country boys being yokels, but a boy's a boy and a man's a man in any place.

Another thing about a village is that if you put a foot wrong everyone knows about it — so you're a bit careful where you tread. But if you do stumble there isn't the condemnation you get in a town. People there live much closer to nature, and they know that when a boy and a girl get together things can and may happen. Mind you, if they did, the parents of the girl, if not of the boy, certainly expected him to marry her. Olive told me that many a girl that got married in white was already on the way to the family way. In fact, some people considered you a bit of a snob if you weren't, after all babies were God's gifts, the way they arrived was only incidental. And, village folk are in contact with the animals that are breeding all the time. In any case there's very little else to do and the opportunities are so profuse, I mean you're wandering round country lanes, there's no lights, it's pitch dark. Opportunity's the great thing, isn't it?

In a town it's vastly different — it's such an impersonal

place, you don't get the same chance to go out as a family; you don't get to know the opposite sex. If you get pregnant the man can slip through the net and you're left with a baby and the reputation 'she goes with everyone'.

I once went to stay with Olive at Ripe. Now I've talked about the social advantages of village life – but living in a town certainly had compensations. To start with the village was three miles from the nearest bus stop, so that meant over an hour's walk with my luggage. There was no water laid on, no electricity or gas, just oil lamps at night, and you washed yourself in an enamel basin on a built-up brick arrangement with a hole to get rid of the water – you tipped it down the hole and it just cascaded on the floor all over your feet if you didn't stand back; I got caught by it the first time. You got water from a well in the garden. There was nothing to wind it up with, you just knelt on the ground and stuck the bucket in. It was full of little squiggly things that looked like tad-poles. Olive said they got boiled before you have them in tea. I thought I wasn't very keen on boiled tadpoles. And everything tasted of smoke. Her mother only had an open fire to cook on.

I shared a bed with Olive, a lovely comfortable bed it was one of these feather mattresses you just shake up. I thought it was the last word in comfort. But there was the most terrible scratching noise going on overhead. I said to Olive, 'What's that?' She said, 'Oh, it's only a rat up in the roof.' *Only* a rat up in the roof! I nearly died. 'Search the roof and get it out,' I demanded. 'It never comes out,' she said, 'it's got a nest up there.' I nearly passed out.

The sanitary arrangements were of the most primitive. They were right down the garden path, and believe me they needed to be. It was the most attractive place in the daylight overgrown with rambler roses, but when you went in! It was one of those awful arrangements which the man every so often had to dig out and bury. And it had one of those seats with two holes. The sort for Darby and Joan who couldn't bear to be separated. Talk about two hearts that beat as one! Heaven knows it was lethal enough when only one had been in. I shouldn't think two could have come out alive.

But it was Olive's home and she was very happy there.

They used to say in towns about villages that everyone knew your business; of course, everybody *does*, but you know their business too, so it's one close-knit community which I think is a good thing. I live in a town, and I couldn't even tell you the names of the people that live two or three doors up the road. Nobody speaks to anybody and it's considered the greatest compliment if you're known as a person who keeps herself to herself. But this kind of attitude doesn't help herself to get herself a himself, does it?

# 21

As TIME went on Lady Gibbons was getting more and more morose. I think by the things she let drop that money was rather tight, and that Sir Walter had made some rather unfortunate investments. Perhaps that was why she was so mean, that there really wasn't very much money.

When Christmas came round I had to cook a turkey and I made a very sad job of it. I couldn't get on with that kitchen range, either I made it too hot, or it wasn't hot enough. This time it was too hot and the turkey got burnt. I scraped it all off as much as I could with the nutmeg grater, I put brown breadcrumbs over the worst of the burns. I hoped for the best and I sent it upstairs. I expected to hear an explosion of rage from Sir Walter, through the service lift. But all was quiet. When Olive came down I said, 'Didn't he say anything?' 'Not a thing,' Olive replied. 'What about her?' I said. Olive said, 'Well, her face changed colour a bit, she turned it around, and she looked at it from all angles, but nothing was said, not from any of them.' So when two or three days had gone by and Lady Gibbons had still said nothing, I began to think that perhaps it had been all right.

But on the fourth morning, out of the blue, old Lady Gibbons said to me, 'Cook, whatever happened to the turkey?' I said, 'Turkey, M'Lady?' She said, 'Yes, turkey.' So I said, 'Well, it did get a bit burned.' So she said, 'A bit burned! It was just like a cinder, and when Sir Walter went to cut it, the flesh just fell off.' I said, 'Well, that's a sign of it being tender.' 'It wasn't a sign of it being tender with your turkey,' she said. 'It's a pity we're not all vegetarians, because that's the only thing you can cook.' So I said, 'Well, your Ladyship, that brings me to a matter I wanted to speak to you about.' I noticed she went pale at this – she thought I was going to give in my notice and that most obviously wouldn't have suited her. Burnt offering was better than no burnt offering. 'It's this,' I said. 'I thought that I might take a few cookery lessons in the afternoons.'

I really had thought about this and the turkey sort of sealed matters. You see it had been my biggest failure and after all turkeys do cost a lot of money. The wretched bird was on my conscience. 'That's a very good idea,' she said, her face relaxing and the colour coming back into it. Then her jaw stiffened. 'But you'll have to pay for them yourself, of course.' That leopard couldn't change her spots either.

I looked around and settled upon a place with the title of 'Léon's Grand School of Continental Cookery'. It was a very imposing building from the outside, though afterwards I discovered that the part he had was very small indeed, just one large room in a very decayed condition. But the lessons were cheap, 2s 6d for a class lesson and 5s for a private one. I took the six class lessons first.

Monsieur Léon was middle-aged with a head of bushy hair which he covered with one of those tall chefs' hats. He certainly looked professional, and there's no getting away from the fact that he was a good cook. He taught us to make some marvellous things out of very little. This pleased Lady Gibbons.

For instance one of the lessons was making puff pastry. It rose as high as I've ever seen pastry rise, and yet he used margarine. Mind you, he never let us taste it which was probably as well.

All the time he was teaching he'd keep up a running commentary like these French people are supposed to do. 'Voilà', he'd say, and 'Comme ci, comme ça', and 'oui, oui'. Well, I didn't even know what they meant, but it sounded frenchy to me, so I took it at its face value.

When I had my first private lesson I went round to the back of his table and got in close contact with his two gas-stoves and the things that were around them. I've never seen anything like it in all my life! There were saucepans galore, with bits of food in them that must have been there from time immemorial, and there was enough penicillin in those saucepans to cure a hospital I should think, if they'd known about penicillin then. The frying-pans were stuck on to the gas stoves by congealed fat and the smell, well the smell just finished me off. 'Monsieur Léon,' I said, 'it's all bloody filthy,' then I fainted, absolutely passed out on the floor.

When I came to Monsieur Léon was bending over me

giving me a drop of brandy, and himself about half a glass. He was talking in a voice from which all trace of French accent had gone. I said to him, 'Monsieur Léon, you're no more French than I am.' 'Course I'm not,' he said, and then under the influence of the brandy he became very confidential. 'I was in the cookhouse in France during the war doing army cooking,' he said. 'That gave me the rudiments of it, then I deserted. I had a girl there, we got married as a matter of fact,' he said. 'Well, she up and left me afterwards, but I'd picked up quite a bit about cooking. Then I came back to England,' he said, 'and I set up this place.' 'What is your real name?' I said. 'Percy Taylor,' he said. 'How could I have started – Percy Taylor's School of Continental Cookery? I wouldn't have got a single pupil, so I called myself Léon and I used some of the French words I'd picked up. I used to know a lot more but I've forgotten them now.' 'Yes,' I thought, 'and you've probably forgotten your French cooking.' Anyway, that was the last time I went to him. Lady Gibbons had to make do with cooking à la Margaret.

One thing she and many like her couldn't abide was breakages. In domestic service breakages are an occupational hazard particularly when you've got a lot of washing-up to do. But no one would recognize this, Lady Gibbons least of all. It was always the same when I dropped anything. 'What is it this time, cook?' I'd tell her. 'Oh no, not that,' as though 'that' was her dearest possession. Now it's a peculiar thing; in all my years of domestic service I noticed that it didn't matter what got broken, it was always something that Madam 'particularly treasured', or it 'cost a lot of money', or it was 'a family heirloom', or it was 'irreplaceable', or it had 'sentimental value'; it was never just an ordinary thing that you could go to the shop and buy. It used to remind me of a furniture remover who was packing china and broke a plate. And the owner said, 'Oh dear, that plate was over a hundred years old,' so the fellow said to her, 'Oh was it? Well, it was high time it went then, wasn't it?'

One morning Lady Gibbons came down and announced that the family would be going into the country for two months, somewhere in Yorkshire, and the house was going to be shut up. She said she'd found another place for Olive with a friend. I was astonished at Olive letting her find a place for her. Nothing would have induced me to work for a friend of Lady Gibbons because very often you find that people's friends are very much like them. She said she was going to take me with them. There was a cook there already and I was to be the house parlourmaid.

All this without so much as 'by your leave', and do you mind having your status changed, and do you mind going to Yorkshire? What did she think I was, some chattel that she could move around? I was determined that nothing on earth would induce me to go to Yorkshire, not even if she was to offer me double money. Not as parlourmaid. I would have suffered agonies of embarrassment having to serve at table; I suffered agonies just going in the room where they were, never mind waiting at table on them.

When I told her I didn't want to leave London she said that this place where they were going was right in the heart of the country, in beautiful surroundings. If only she'd have known that settled it for me. I'd had enough of the country when I stayed at Olive's place.

I could imagine Yorkshire. I visualized some spot right in the middle of the moors, and me stuck there with old Sir Walter and Lady Gibbons. I disliked the country in any case, for when you've seen one cow, or one tree, you've seen them all in my opinion. A cow's got four legs, a tree's got branches, but they don't do anything, do they? I like talk, people, and things that move around with a purpose.

When old Lady Gibbons realized that I was determined not to go, she wanted to get me a temporary job; you see she wanted someone to come back to. The fact that otherwise she'd have to give me a whole eight weeks' holiday with pay was nearly killing her. Anyway I said, 'Well, I'm very sorry, M'Lady, I don't care for temporary work. I'll take it, but if the position suits I would feel I would have to stay. So I shouldn't rely on me being here when you get back.' That was enough for her, I knew she wouldn't let me go.

She didn't say anything then, she had to make it look as if *she*'d made the decision, but the next day she came down, and said that Sir Walter and she had thought that under the circumstances it would be better not to shut the house down, and that I could stay to keep an eye on it; I could live at home if I wanted to. She would pay me my wages and fifteen shillings a week board. That was just fine. I got two months' holiday with pay. Something unheard of. I was in the seventh heaven.

The strange part was that when she came back I only stayed another four months. Perhaps I'd got used to not working there. When I gave in my notice I said that the doctor felt it wasn't good for my health living in a dark basement with the light on all day.

When you gave in your notice, you always tried to give the impression that you were loath to leave, you just had to make it seem that you were sorry to go. It was because of the reference; you couldn't get another job without a good reference. Nowadays, of course, people forge them. If I'd have known anything about it, I would have forged mine. It's all my eye and Betty Martin that they should rely on what the last person you worked for said. She might try to spite you because you left her. If people were the soul of honour, whether they liked you or not, they'd give you a good reference if you deserved it, but people just aren't like that. I don't know whether Lady Gibbons swallowed my story but she did give me quite a good reference, she didn't praise me up to the skies, but she said I was honest, hard working, and a good cook. What more could I expect?

# 22

AFTER I'D finished at Lady Gibbons' I decided to try temporary work for a change. I thought that by doing temporary work I wouldn't stay long wherever I went, that I'd do lots of different jobs in a short time and that in that way I'd get a lot of experience. It's very seldom that two people have the same ideas about cooking. Some people like made-up dishes, other people like plain food, some are particular about sweets, others about savouries. So I thought I'd quickly gain knowledge and experience by doing a variety of jobs.

It didn't work out like that. I discovered that generally the people who advertised for a temporary cook only did so because no self-respecting cook would ever stay with them permanently. The first job I took was at Stanley Gardens in Notting Hill Gate.

In recent years it's become notorious because of a murder that was done there. At the time I was there it was a collection of large, ugly Victorian houses that were already going seedy.

The people I worked for were Jewish, a Mr and Mrs Bernard. They weren't orthodox Jews, although they didn't eat pork or bacon, but they didn't observe all the things that orthodox Jews do, like keeping all the teacloths and the cutlery and utensils used for milk separate. Later on in my life as a cook, I worked for two other Jewish families who were very generous but Mr and Mrs Bernard certainly didn't fit into that category. They were just plain mean, and made Lady Gibbons seem like Lady Bountiful, though they were more easygoing than she was.

For example, my bedroom and the bedrooms of the house-maid and parlourmaid were furnished with an absolute minimum. Beds were rock hard, and for blankets we had plush curtains with all the bobbles still hanging on them. I had green, and the other two had red. The quilt had been cut in half so that there was a fringe one side and the other that went by the wall was just a plain hem. There was one chair, and a corner fitment to hang clothes, not a wardrobe, just a few hooks with a curtain across. Then a washstand with a broken leg propped up by books.

Mrs Bernard suffered with phlebitis, and she was for ever complaining about it and showing her leg to all and sundry. It used to drive me up the wall. When I went to bed at night I used to try to creep up the stairs like a mouse, because if she heard me passing her bedroom she'd call out, 'Who's there? Oh it's you, cook, come in.' And I used to have to go and gaze at this horrible leg that she spread out on the bed. It was a most unlovely sight. All swollen up, like a bladder of lard. I suppose I should have felt sorry for her, it must have been painful and certainly she couldn't get around very well. But I couldn't because of this constant parading of her woes, and the very sight of her opulent bedroom and the comparison with ours used to infuriate me. There she'd sit all day in bed eating chocolates and displaying her leg. I think she got to be proud of it. Anyway she felt it was part of our job to look sympathetic.

Edna, the parlourmaid, had to take up a brown roll and a pat of butter last thing just in case she got hungry in the night. If it wasn't eaten, she used to send it down for us in the kitchen. But I'd never use it for the simple reason that this brown roll and butter used to stand on the night commode. Talk about hygiene!

Mr Bernard was a benevolent-looking old gentleman, but this benevolence was only superficial. They talk about beauty only being skin deep, but benevolence is only skin deep, believe me. If Mrs Bernard couldn't come down to the kitchen to give her orders, Mr Bernard used to come down. He always tried to get me into a confined space, like the larder or the scullery, and then he'd put his hand on my arm, or shoulder, and his fingers were as bony as a bank-clerk's. 'Shall we work out the menu?' he used to say. I don't know where he thought the menu was. Then he'd hang over my shoulder while I wrote. I wouldn't have minded this weak display of amorousness if there had been anything attached to it, like a pair of stockings or a box of chocolates, but there never was. He didn't want to do anything more than fondle your neck, I know, but there's no pleasure in that from an old man, is there?

He used to do the shopping. Every morning he'd go to the Portobello Market. If we wanted a salad he'd bring back a lettuce and a beetroot, or a lettuce and tomatoes. Never anything else. To make a salad with. I ask you. He said it provided scope for ingenuity. But even ingenuity requires some raw materials, doesn't it? I wasn't a miracle worker. I wonder he didn't bring the water down to see if I could turn it into wine for them.

The trouble was they couldn't afford to keep three maids, but the house was of a size that couldn't be run with less than three. Even as it was, nothing really got done as it should have been done. Everything looked old and shabby, except for her bedroom and the drawing-room.

In the kitchen there were just worn linoleum, shapeless wicker chairs, an ancient kitchen stove, and all the utensils were worn out and the implements, like the brooms and brushes, were always losing their hairs, and nothing ever got replaced. I'm not surprised they advertised for temporary maids. They knew they wouldn't keep them for any time.

I stayed for three months and the only good I got from it was that it was there I invented my famous kipper savoury. It was funny the way this happened. One morning we had kippers for breakfast, and Mrs Bernard, who always had her breakfast in bed, didn't eat hers. When Ethel brought the tray down I threw the kipper into the pig bucket under the sink. But when Mr Bernard came down to give the orders he said, 'Cook, Madam would like you to make her a savoury for dinner tonight using that kipper that she left from breakfast.' My heart sank. I didn't dare say I'd thrown it away because if I had it would have ruined the day for both of them, and I didn't see why I should ruin someone's day over a kipper. So I just said, 'Oh yes, Sir, that'll be all right.' As soon as he'd gone upstairs I rushed to the pig bucket and I fished the kipper out. It was covered in tea leaves and some other nasty bits and pieces. So I rinsed it under the tap. Unfortunately as I rinsed, I was washing up at the time, it fell into my bowl of washing-up water and soap suds. So I fished it out again and hastily gave it another rinse, and I kept smelling it to see if the soap had gone. At last I thought it had. Then the problem was what to do with it to make sure it didn't taste of soap suds. Anyway I got all the flesh off and pounded it well in the pestle and mortar, and I used that good old stand-by, Escoffier sauce. It's a marvellous thing for disguising the flavour of something you don't want noticed. I sent it up well garnished and decorated, and to my surprise Mrs Bernard sent the parlourmaid down with a compliment. She said, 'Tell cook that's the most delicious savoury we've ever eaten.' I thought, 'That's it, girl. When you want real flavours stir things around in the pig bucket first.'

As you can imagine I hadn't been there long before I realized I'd got all the knowledge I was ever likely to get from them. So I left. The next job that I took was with a Lord and Lady Downall in Chelsea.

The contrast was fantastic. They were the most thoughtful and kind people I'd ever met, ever since I started in domestic service. Unfortunately *they*'d advertised for a temporary because they really needed one. Their own cook was in hospital and was only going to be away three months. They were so pleasant and unassuming in their contact with us that I think for the first time since I started work, I lost the feeling that we were a race apart, and that the gap between us and them was unbridgeable. They spoke to us in exactly the same way that they would speak to people of their own society.

For instance we were all called by our Christian names. And it was the first place that *I*'d been in where the people above – 'Them' – called you by your Christian name.

And the servants' hall was an absolute revelation to me. This one was comfortably furnished and it had a colour scheme to it. We had comfortable armchairs, a carpet on the floor, a standard lamp, and other small lamps around, pictures and ornaments. Things that you could tell were bought specially for us, not cast-offs from their rooms. Things that really matched instead of a room full of bits from the conservatory, bits from the drawing-room, and bits from the dining-room. The whole room was welcoming, so that when you had spare time you felt you could really relax even though you were still on duty.

We all had a colour scheme in our bedrooms, mine was green. I had a green carpet, a green eiderdown, and green blankets with satin bindings, and it was absolutely fantastic – a bedside lamp and a table.

Everything was done to make you feel that they really cared about you. All Lady Downall's servants had been with her for many years, and none of them had any intention of leaving.

As I've said, the reason I was there was because her own

cook was in hospital. And when she was ready to leave the hospital she was to be sent away to convalesce for a month at Lady Downall's own expense. To be taken care of for a whole month! Such things were a revelation to me.

And when it was the servants' birthdays they all had lovely presents, not print dresses, black stockings, and caps and things like that, but real presents. Things that they wouldn't have thought of buying themselves. Just to show you how good they were, my birthday came round six weeks after I got there, and *I* got a present. I hadn't told Lady Downall, she must have found out for herself, and she bought me beautiful silk underwear, the sort of thing I'd never been able to buy. Yet I'd only been there six weeks and she knew I was only going to stay three months, but it didn't make any difference.

It could have been that they were the real aristocracy. I think the name was very old.

Lord Downall had been something in India, like so many of the people I'd worked for. He must have been a big pot then. I never did find out what he did or had been. He was a very tall man, six foot three, extremely aristocratic-looking. He had eyes that sort of could see right inside you.

I remember the first time I met him. I happened to pass him on the stairs, and he stopped, and he said to me, 'Oh,' he said, 'are you our new cook?' and I said, 'Yes, Sir,' you know, colouring up like a beetroot, and he said, 'Well, I hope you'll be happy here. You'll find it's a very happy house.' And he was right, it was. The parlourmaid said to me, 'You ought to be here at Christmas. We have a simply wonderful time at

Christmas,' she said. 'We have our own tree and our own presents, all put round the tree,' she said, 'none of this business of having to go up there and parade in front of them. They're all put there overnight,' she said. 'We can go to a theatre during the month of January, any theatre that you choose, and you don't have to go together, you can take your own friend.'

I didn't wonder that Lady Downall never had a servant problem. There the servants really cared about their employers. If anyone had said that to me before I'd have said, 'Oh, that's my eye, no one cares about the people they work for. You work for them and you do the best you can because they're paying you, and because you like to make a good job, but you can't care about them.'

I got four pounds a month there too. You know I didn't wish their poor cook any harm, but I couldn't help hoping that she'd get complications and be away for a year or so. It's terrible, isn't it, to be like that, but I was so happy there.

And it was so pleasant when Lady Downall came down in the mornings; she'd say, 'Good morning, Margaret. Have you any suggestions for lunch?' in a pleasant tone of voice. Or, 'Oh Margaret, as there'll be such a large dinner party we'll have a cold lunch today. That'll give you more time for the preparation tonight.' Consideration, you see. A rare quality.

This gave me the incentive to cook as well and better than I had done. One of my specialities was soufflés. I used to make marvellous soufflés, I had a light hand in those days. Either savoury ones, or sweet ones. But I could never do much with them on those kitchen ranges. Either they got too hot and the soufflé shot up like mad before the centre was cooked, or else it never rose at all. I'd battled for so many years with kitchen ranges that I got a thing about them and used to look on them as my bitterest enemy. But there I had a gas stove and I was fine.

Every night when I went to bed there I used to pore over Mrs Beeton's cookery book. That was the book we all used in those days. I'd pick out a recipe and study it well so that when Lady Downall said next day, 'Have you any suggestions?' I could produce this recipe, sort of casual like, as though it had been a thing I'd done often. I used to work it out in my imagination until the dish was absolute perfection. In my mind that is, not always on the table. Still that happens to all cooks, we all plan things, but they don't always quite work out as we hope they will. Lady Downall used to appreciate any suggestions, and once she said to me, 'You know, I'm very fond indeed of old Aggie' (that was her real cook) 'and she's been with us for years, she started as kitchen maid in my mother's house, but it has been a very pleasant change having all these different things that you know how to do.'

Little did she know I'd sat up half the night before, learning them.

Lady Downall loved going to the Caledonian Market. It's closed now, but at that time it was thriving in Camden Town. She used to love wandering around looking at the genuine antiques, well, that's what they told you they were; genuine antiques. We used to take it in turn to go with her, and great fun it was. The chauffeur used to bring the car round about ten o'clock. I sat in front with him.

He was a very handsome man, not that I could do much about it because Lady Downall could see if you were laughing too much or anything. Anyway, the fact that he was handsome couldn't mean that much because he was already snaffled. He was married and had two children.

We used to wander around the market, and Lady Downall would pick out any items that she fancied and that she thought were good. She never bargained for them because she said immediately she opened her mouth she put her foot in it. She meant that if she asked about the price they knew that she'd got money, and they put their prices up accordingly. So if she saw anything she fancied, she would get whoever she had taken with her to go up and ask the price, and bargain for it.

I remember once while she was looking to see what *she* fancied, I was wandering around to see if there was anything I fancied, and I noticed on one stall a very large blue pot with a handle each side. I thought to myself, that would be just fine for my mother's aspidistra – everyone had an aspidistra in those days. So I approached the stall-holder in what I thought was a nonchalant manner; mind you, they know perfectly well you've got your eye on something, they weren't born yesterday. But I looked at everything but this pot, and I thought I was being very clever. At last I said to him, 'How much is that blue pot?' so he said, 'Oh, ten bob to you,' so I said, 'How much to anyone else, half a crown I suppose? I'll give you five shillings for it.' So he said, 'Five bob? You must be joking. Anyway, what do you want it for?' I told him I wanted it for my mother's aspidistra. 'Good idea,' he said, 'and when she's finished using it for that, she can knock one handle off and stick it under her bed! Two things for the price of one. You've got a good ten bob's worth there, haven't you?' I blushed like a beetroot, and beat a hasty retreat. I never went near that stall again!

# 23

ALL TOO quickly those three months passed. Perhaps flushed with my success at Lady Downall's I decided I'd try one more temporary job.

I got a place near Victoria Station. It was one of those grim, tall, rather shabby houses outside, with an interior to match. It was one of those 'I'm here for ever' kind of houses.

Here again we were underfed and underlodged. For the first and last time in my life I slept on chaff. The mattress was made of chaff, and laid on lathes, you know, not on a spring at all. As I moved in the night it rustled as though I was a horse turning over. Even at home we had flock beds that you could shake up and make comfortable.

I didn't sleep a wink on my first night, and when I got up in the morning I was determined to complain about the bed. But at ten o'clock when my employer, Mrs Hunter-Jones her name was (Hunter-Jones, hyphenated you know, you must always sound the two together), when she appeared she looked so formidable that all my resolutions to moan about it faded away completely. I just hadn't got the pluck to say a word. It's terrible to be a coward like that but one look at her face finished me. I comforted myself with the thought that I wasn't serving a life sentence, I had only gone there as a temporary, and temporary I now decided it was going to be.

The housemaid and the parlourmaid, they'd been there two years, but as their ages were sixty-three and sixty-five it wasn't easy for them to find other employment. Conditions were beginning to get a little bit better – not that people had suddenly changed and become more humane, but there were now more occupations for women to choose from, and naturally if there was other work they could do instead of domestic service they did it. So there was some competition and this meant providing better conditions. But at the ages of sixty- three and sixty-five domestic service was the *only* thing left to do.

For these two poor old things years of spinsterhood and working in other people's houses had made their hands bent, their faces all craggy, and their dispositions extremely foul. And the appearance of these blighted specimens of womanhood plus that of the formidable Mrs Hunter-Jones made me determined to leave at the earliest opportunity. You see all the time I was thinking I might get married, that was my main object in life, and every new job I got I thought somebody might come along, perhaps one of the tradesmen might be all right, and that would be that.

But I could see that this house was a dead duck from that point of view straight away, and the idea of getting experience as a temporary wasn't going to work either because Mr and

Mrs Hunter-Jones did no entertaining at all, and the plainness of the food was only equalled by the scarcity of it. So with no pleasure in cooking, no company but those two old drears, and a house that was as quiet as a mausoleum, I was very depressed.

Even if you've got a mistress who's disagreeable, if the other servants are young and lively you can extract some humour from the place even if it's only making a combined attack on her upstairs. We used to give them a sort of kitchen psycho-analysis, Freud wasn't in it. Mind you I reckoned we knew more about their sex life than he'd ever have discovered.

But that subject would have been out even if my gaunt companions could have discussed it. It's my confident opinion that the old dear could never have indulged; she hadn't any children and a look at her husband would have confirmed my view. He was a trophy, if the truth was known, and he might just as well have hung on the wall with the other antlers for all the use he could have been.

But not only was there no congenial company in this house, there was nowhere to sit and relax. There wasn't even a servants' hall. You just sat in the kitchen surrounded by the 'Ideal' boiler, the gas stove, the kitchen table, and the dresser. So I took to going out of an evening.

I had a friend, she only lived about ten minutes' walk away, who was also in service. I used to go out and see her about half past eight, but I was always in before ten o'clock. It didn't hurt anyone at all. But it didn't please those other two old servants. I know they were sour, but you wouldn't have thought they would have moaned about it because after all it didn't affect them. But the thing was *they* couldn't get out, so why should I be able to?

So after I'd been out a few nights they informed Mrs Hunter-Jones. This information was a great shock to her. She had never heard of such a thing as a servant going out above the stipulated time for her outings, so I had to listen to a long lecture, and demands as to why I wanted to go out of an evening. She said, 'You have every Sunday evening and one other evening free.' 'Yes, Madam,' I replied, 'but when I finish work there's nowhere comfortable to sit.' So she said, 'Oh well, other cooks have sat in the kitchen, why cannot you? You're certainly not free to go out whenever you feel like it.'

I thought about this and I thought about these two old spinsters. It didn't really make me dislike them because I could see that their lives were unhappy.

Their names were Violet and Lily, names which probably suited them some forty years ago, but it certainly didn't go at all well with their appearance or their dispositions now.

On one of the rare occasions when we all got chummy together they'd told me that they'd worked as a parlourmaid and a housemaid for twenty-five years in the same house for one lady, a childless widow. According to Lily and Violet, this lady had promised them that if they stayed with her until she died she'd leave them an annuity, enough money for them to leave domestic service and set up a flat together. Mind you, I thought they were muggins not to have seen the proof. Anyway, when the old lady did die it was found she hadn't made a will at all, and all the money went to her next-of-kin, her nephew. He just sold the house, and all poor Violet and Lily got was three months' wages, and then he thought he was being very generous to them, because nothing stipulated that he should give them anything.

So you can imagine after twenty-five years in one job, and what they thought was coming at the end of it, then to be dismissed with three months' wages. You can't wonder that they were grim, can you?

Mind you, it happened in a lot of cases. It was a way of keeping servants when you were getting old. But it's hopeless to trust in people like that. I wouldn't have believed a word.

The trouble was that they were convinced that their madam had really left them the money and that the nephew had done them out of it. I tried to explain to them about wills and solicitors and things, but they didn't want to believe me. Well, nobody likes to think that they've been caught for a sucker, do they? But it made me understand why they were so sour and everything.

It was only too evident they would never get anything from Mrs Hunter-Jones. She underpaid them anyway because she knew that they'd have difficulty getting a job anywhere else.

Still I didn't feel that by staying in the house I could alleviate their lot in any way. There'd just be three disgruntled people instead of two. So I gave Mrs Hunter-Jones a month's notice. It was a very unpleasant business working out my notice in that house. A month is a long time when people are unpleasant to you, and the two old dears, although I didn't make things any worse for them, resented that I could get out, that I'd got a future, and that they hadn't. They'd only got the past and that hadn't been too good.

My main worry was about my reference, because I sensed that Mrs Hunter-Jones wouldn't give me a good one in spite of the fact that I came to her with a wonderful recommendation from Lady Downall. I tried to get a written one from her so that I could read her opinion of me, and then perhaps I could have done something about it. But she wouldn't give me one, she said she never reckoned to do anything like that.

It was with some considerable trepidation that I gave the next prospective employer Mrs Hunter-Jones' telephone number. I knew they wouldn't meet each other because I had decided that I would work in Brighton for a while, so at least I knew that they wouldn't get together and have a good natter over me.

The job I went after was in The Drive which at that time was a very palatial road indeed. I was interviewed by a Mrs Bishop. I took great pains to tell her I'd only been temporary at Mrs Hunter-Jones', but she said that she would ring her up and would I call back the next day to see what the verdict was.

When I went she said, 'What a peculiar person your last employer is. When I telephoned her for a reference she said, "Well, I think Margaret Langley could cook if she was ever in to cook, but as she expects to be out morning, afternoon, and evening, she never has the time."' That reference would have been damning in the ordinary way but it turned out that Mrs Bishop had an odd way of life which made it difficult for her to get and keep a staff.

So in spite of Mrs Hunter-Jones' efforts she engaged me as a cook at a wage of fifty-two pounds a year. This was very good money indeed because this was not temporary, it was a permanent job.

You may think I'm going on about this reference business. But it was most frightfully important then. People were frightened that you might steal things or that you might be working 'inside' for a gang of thieves. They wanted to know all the ins and outs about you. Mind you, they never gave you a reference about themselves, which I used to think you had a right to; whether you had to work like a slave, whether they kept late hours, whether they were mean and selfish, whether they treated you like dirt; nothing like that, but they wanted to know all about you. And if you hadn't got a good reference from your last place it was useless to explain that you'd been in domestic service since you were fifteen years old, that there were many other people to whom they could apply, and that the reason that this reference wasn't a good one was because in your last place you dared to speak up about conditions of employment. Employers didn't want to hear that kind of thing. That was bolshevism. 'How dare one of the lower classes criticize the upper classes!' Girls like me who they considered came from poverty-stricken homes should be glad to work in a large house with food and warmth. To them upstairs, any home was better than the one that you lived in with your parents. It was mutiny if you said in your last place you didn't have this or that – it must have been better than what you've been used to. And as for domestic servants having aspirations to rise above the basement, such a thing was incredible to them.

Even Lady Downall was the same in some respects. I remember asking her if I could borrow a book from her library to read, and I can see now the surprised look on her face. She said, 'Yes, of course, certainly you can, Margaret,' adding, 'but I didn't know you read.' They knew that you breathed and you slept and you worked, but they didn't know that you *read*. Such a thing was beyond comprehension. They thought that in your spare time you sat and gazed into space, or looked at *Peg's Paper* or the *Crimson Circle*. You could almost see them reporting you to their friends. 'Margaret's a good cook, but unfortunately she reads. Books, you know.'

# 24

THE BISHOPS' house was a large, four-storeyed, detached building with the usual basement, and a back stairs for the servants.

Mrs Bishop was an absolute revelation to me. I had been used to solid superficial respectability, with 'Them' upstairs. But what a change she was. She was Italian by birth, nearly sixty years old, but made-up to look about thirty, and from the back view that's the age she looked. She had her face enamelled, I don't quite know what they did with it, but she never gave a hearty laugh, she just tittered so that it never cracked. She didn't move the muscles of her face. Her hair was dyed, and hair-dyeing in those days hadn't reached the perfection it has now, so that each subsequent dye was never the same colour as the last, and the head became patchy. I couldn't take my eyes off her when we first met. She had a figure slim like a young girl's. That was unusual in those days. People weren't figure-conscious, nobody thought of dieting. They merrily consumed three-course lunches, and five- or six-course dinners every day, and 'hang your figure'. She had an attractive husky voice. I thought she had a sore throat when she interviewed me. She was very proud of this voice, she said, 'It's just like Tallulah Bankhead's, you know.' Tallulah Bankhead was all the vogue at that time.

As well as the house they had a flat in London. They spent from Tuesday afternoon to Friday afternoon there. This meant that, although we had free time in the week, we never had a weekend to ourselves. This was the reason she had difficulty getting maids because they like their free days at weekends, especially if they happen to be courting. But it didn't worry me, I hadn't got a young man yet.

From Friday evening until Monday morning the house used to be packed with visitors, some were young business people, a lot were hangers-on of the film and theatre world, nobody of any class at all, always plenty of young men of a variety of nationalities. Mrs Bishop was very very fond of young men. None of us ever had half an hour we could call our own at weekends. I didn't mind at all, at least there was some life, even if I was getting it second hand.

In this somewhat bizarre household I used to have to go and get my orders while Mrs Bishop was in the bath. I was horrified at first because I'd never seen a nude figure, not even a woman, before. It was amazing, after a couple of weeks I got quite used to it, and I'd sit on the edge of the bath, while she used to tell me what she wanted.

One morning at ten o'clock I went to the bathroom. I'd got so used to going there I just used to knock and walk in without waiting for an answer. On this particular morning, to my horror, instead of seeing a very flat, nude, white body lying there, there was a huge, black, hairy one, standing up in the bath. It was an Italian. Well, it was the first time I'd ever seen a full-scale appendage in my life. And after having had a look at it I could quite see why Adam rushed to get a fig leaf! I would have too if I'd discovered I had an object like that! The shock! It took me about a week to get over this thing. Mind you, he didn't think anything of me seeing him at all. He told Madam afterwards that he'd like to come down and apologize to me. Thank heaven he didn't. After seeing him in the nude I couldn't possibly have seen him clothed. I should have been visualizing it all the time.

I remember the other maids, they wanted to know about it in detail, and everything. They said, 'I bet you rushed out,' 'I bet you had a good look.' Things like that had more importance in those days. Anyway, from then on I never went in without knocking and waiting to make sure it was Mrs Bishop who answered.

Young men were Mrs Bishop's life. They say life begins at forty, well she must have had twenty years of hard living. Mind you, she wasn't unattractive, her face was skilfully made up and we always had the blinds at half-mast. It gave her subdued light, and that helped.

She used to have some furious rows with these young men and I'd know that, when I saw her the next morning, I'd be in for a tearful session. She'd give me the same old routine over and over again, I must have heard it more than a dozen times. 'Oh, you know, Margaret,' she said, 'I was married straight from the convent, when I was seventeen years old, and I never saw Mr Bishop until I stood before the altar with him. I never had a chance to live when I was young, I was married to a man ten years older than me and I saw nothing of the world at all, and now it's too late.' Well, naturally, I had to agree with her. She didn't want my opinion, she just wanted my sympathy. I couldn't see that she'd made such a bad bargain, she had a lovely house, servants, jewels, and a life of ease; I mean if that wasn't living, it was a bloody good imitation. I'd have married Old Nick himself for the sort of life she had.

Mr Bishop was a different kettle of fish altogether. I think he was of German origin and had changed his name during the war. He had a very placid temperament. Of course, they lived entirely separate lives, she slept on one floor, the second floor, he was on the floor above and they had very little to do with each other. They went up to London together and they came back together, but they weren't married in the true sense of the word when I knew them; that was finished.

I liked him. He certainly had a sense of humour. While they were up in London we used to take the run of the house; use their sitting-room, play all their records, and I used to bang out tunes on the piano. One day there I caught my hand in the car rack and nearly broke my thumb. I had to be taken to the doctor's and have it bandaged. When I passed Mr Bishop the next day he said to me, 'How's your thumb getting along, cook?' and I said, 'Oh it's all right, Sir. It's a bit difficult to work with.' He said, 'Yes, and a bit difficult to play the piano, too, isn't it?' Someone must have told him what we did when they weren't there, but he said it with a twinkle. He didn't mind.

Still after all, this was mild stuff compared with what he was putting up with from Mrs Bishop. He turned a blind eye to that too. I heard that twice she had tried to commit suicide or staged a suicide by taking too many pills or something, and that one of the sons was a 'ticket of leave man' in Australia, as they called them: he was sent two pounds a week to keep him out there. I think he'd forged his father's name to a cheque. So he'd had his troubles in his time and wasn't looking for any more. They weren't of course what you could call the gentry.

But it was lively, you see. Every now and again when she had some Italian friends Mrs Bishop would come down to the kitchen and say, did I mind if they came down and made some special Italian dishes? I didn't mind because they were nearly always young people. Mind you, they made a hell of a mess and used to leave the kitchen in a filthy state; it didn't occur to them to do the washing-up. But I used to watch them and get all the pointers that I could. So although I couldn't say I was working for the 'quality', I couldn't care less. I got my money, had a gay, amusing life, and that was all that mattered to me.

One of these young men who was her favourite longer than anyone else was one of these Italians. Proper ice-cream man. He used to walk round with a little monkey on his shoulder, I used to be terrified. Mrs Bishop provided him with money; he was what you call a gigolo. He wasn't a day over twenty-five, and with her being sixty she probably didn't provide him with much else. So if he could find one of the young maids to have a little interlude with, he would. He'd come down to the kitchen with his foul monkey on his shoulder and he'd try to get you in conversation. He'd start off about food and that kind of thing, and go on to, 'Have you got a boyfriend?' I don't know why they ask you that. Then he'd edge round the table towards you, and I would keep edging farther and farther away, because I knew perfectly well that whatever his intentions were, they certainly weren't honourable. He never got anywhere with me. It just wasn't worth your while wasting your time on impossibles, all your efforts were needed to allure the possibles, the ones who might have good intentions.

I read in the paper the other day that the surplus of young men to girls in England today between the ages of sixteen and twenty-one is fifty-six thousand. It makes me see red. Because then in Brighton, there were five girls to every young man, so you can just imagine what a fight you had to have to get one and keep him. And we never had a free weekend, which was the only time a young man had got any money. By the time we met them they were dead broke, anyway. And if you said you were in domestic service it was still the same old story, you could see their faces change. The less polite ones used to say, 'Oh, skivvies!' and clear off, and leave you cold.

I remember one night Hilda, the parlourmaid, and I went to a dance. Hilda used to stuff her young men up with the idea that she was a secretary. This particular night we collected two naval officers. Of all the snooty fellows in the world, officers from the Royal Navy are the snootiest. I don't know what rank they were, probably the lowest that they could be, consistent with being officers. They were mean as well as snooty because they brought us back on the bus; no taxis. I never pretended to be anything else but the cook because it was always my fate to get a bit of supper for them. I thought that perhaps my way to a man was through his stomach. We used to take them in to the kitchen, you see; we weren't supposed to, but you've got to make up for not having weekends off. Just after we got in Hilda went upstairs to the lavatory and her officer came up to me and said, 'She's not a secretary.' I said, 'Well, she's whatever she says she is,' to cover up for her. 'Well, she's certainly not a secretary, she's the parlour-maid.' I said, 'How do you know?' He said, 'I took her into that place where there's a sink' (he meant the butler's pantry) 'and before she'd let me lay a finger on her she washed up the silver.' You see, she didn't think, she was so used to never letting the silver lie around dirty she had to wash it up. Well, no secretary would have done that, of course. Mind you no officer and a gentleman would have mentioned it. Poor Hilda never joined that branch of the Navy.

Still she had aspirations.

Anyway, life wasn't too hard there for me, there was an odd-job man to do the boiler and the front steps and the boots and shoes. The kitchen floor there was very good, it was paved with smooth red tiles and all you had to do was just wipe them over with a damp cloth. The usual enormous dresser that we always had was fitted with glass cupboards so that nothing got dusty. And there was a telephone in the kitchen.

After that previous place with Mrs Hunter-Jones, it was a great pleasure to be able to cook things like salmon steaks, and jugged hare, and to make real mayonnaise, instead of white sauce. We had things like sirloins and saddles, and I had the opportunity to practise and to learn cooking.

Although I was now quite expert, it was a good job I had never taken up any other part of domestic service like being a parlourmaid and waiting at table. I only had one experience of it and that was enough. One evening Mrs Bishop was giving a dinner party and Hilda was taken ill and couldn't wait at table. Mrs Bishop came rushing down to me to ask if I could come in between the courses and help hand things round. The housemaid was to do the silver serving, and I was to hand the vegetables round. I knew I would suffer agonies of embarrassment. You can just imagine coming up from the heat of the kitchen with a face like a peony and wearing a print dress into the bargain. When I arrived in the dining-room Mrs Bishop announced to the company at large, 'This is my cook.' Well, of course, everybody gaped at me, which didn't help, I felt like exhibit A. One of the vegetables was tiny little new potatoes, they looked very attractive in the dish on the silver salver, with mint and butter sauce – piping hot they were too. The first guest I had to serve was an attractive Frenchwoman. Well, I was so nervous my hand started shaking like a leaf – the dish shot down the salver and all these marble-sized new potatoes shot all down her front and her lap. She jumped up and let out a stream of French words I couldn't understand. Then I saw that one of the potatoes had got lodged in her cleavage – so I tried to get it out with the serving spoon. The silly thing didn't keep still – it must have been burning her – anyway, instead of getting it out I squashed it against her breast. She flung the spoon out of my hand and screamed, 'Coshon, coshon' about half a dozen times. Talk about Oliver Twist, but she didn't ask for more. I fled downstairs.

About a week later when I thought the excitement had died down, I asked Mrs Bishop what this word 'coshon' meant. I thought it must have been something terrible. She said, 'Oh well,' she said, 'it's just a French word that means the same as damn does in English.' It was some years later that I looked it up in a French dictionary, it was spelt C.O.C.H.O.N., I found, and it means you're a pig or a swine. I didn't mind – she got the potatoes. I didn't.

Occasionally during the week Mr Bishop would come down from London. He had a girlfriend I think, in Brighton somewhere, we never saw her but we always assumed that was what he came for. He would always telephone to let us know that he was on his way so that he never caught us in any embarrassing situations. If he ever wanted dinner we never had to worry, he always had the same thing; giblet soup, we always had giblets because there were always chickens in the house; grilled sprats; and stewed pig's trotters. He used to pick up the old trotter and suck away at it. It was the same meal every time, that's what he liked, didn't want anything else.

If we were going dancing we didn't have to give it up, because this was supposed to be our free time. We used to arrange his dinner between us, the housemaid, the parlourmaid, and me. One of us would get on with his dinner while the other one would be getting ready for the dance, so sometimes he got a different person serving each course. Hilda would take in the giblet soup, then she rushed to change, so then the housemaid would go in with the grilled sprats, and then she would tear off, and I would rush up with the trotters. He never seemed to mind.

It was after I had been there some months I discovered that he had a most peculiar aberration. If he came down to the house on his own, he'd always ring the bell in his bedroom at about half past eleven at night, after we'd gone to bed. It rang upstairs on the landing outside the bedrooms, and Hilda or Iris, the housemaid, would slip on a dressing- gown and go down to his room. Then he'd ask them to bring him a whisky and soda, or a jug of water, or even a book that he'd left in the library. I said to Hilda one night, 'Why does he always wait until we've all got in bed before he rings that bell?' So she said, 'It's because he likes to see us in hair curlers.' I said, astonished, 'What do you mean?' She said, 'He likes to see us in hair curlers.' People in those days didn't have hair rollers like nowadays, they were all those dinky steel curlers, and we did our hair up every night in them because it was the fashion to have a mass of frizz, and the bigger you could make it stick out the better it was, you see. So I said, 'You're joking.' 'No, it's the truth,' she said. I said, 'Well, what does he do then when you go in wearing these curlers?' So she said, 'Well, he doesn't really do anything much. He asks us to take off our hair nets and then he fingers the curlers in our hair, you see.' I just couldn't believe it, it seemed pointless, stupid. I said, 'Is that all? He feels your hair curlers?' She said, 'Yes, that's all he does. And he's always happy and pleased when he does it,' she said. She just sat on the edge of his bed and he just felt her hair curlers, and that's all. Well, it struck me then, and it does now, as a most peculiar way of getting pleasure. It just didn't make sense, I mean whoever heard of anyone wanting to see anyone in hair curlers, never mind about feeling them? But Hilda and Iris did quite well from this peculiarity of his, because they used to get cosmetics or boxes of chocolates or stockings each time.

I could have got them as well if I liked. He wouldn't have cared who answered the bell at all so long as you went in your dressing-gown and your hair curlers, but I would never go. Not that I cared whether or not he saw me in hair curlers; I wouldn't let a young man see me, it would be absolute death to a romance and a possible home-provider, but it wouldn't have mattered about him. No, the reason I wouldn't go was because it was yet another demonstration of servants' inferiority. You see he wouldn't have dreamt of asking guests in the house if he could feel their hair curlers. But servants, they should be quite happy in his view because they got presents for doing it. But Hilda and Iris wouldn't agree with me over this; they said, 'Well, what does it matter, it doesn't do us any harm and we get something out of it.' I tried to make them see this, because they had aspirations, not that that got them anywhere. But Iris said, 'So we *are* servants, aren't we?' she said. 'And anything we can get given us for doing nothing at all is so much to the good.' And Hilda she said, 'I get quite a kick out of it, and when I'm waiting at table,' she said, 'and when Mr Bishop is sitting there talking so high-falutin' to his guests,' she said, 'I often feel like slipping a hair curler on his plate!' But I never heard of such a peculiar aberration in my life as hair curlers. I wonder what was the cause of it? Something tied up with his youth I expect, perhaps his mother had them or something.

# 25

ABOUT THIS time I thought I'd managed to snaffle a permanent young man; as you must have gathered, it was no easy task at all with so few opportunities around. This particular one was a window cleaner. When he used to come to clean the windows I'd ask him down to the kitchen and give him tea and cakes made by me, do myself up, and try my hardest to make an impression. They say the way to a man's heart is through his stomach, but believe me, it's mighty hard going at times, some of them have got pretty tough stomachs.

Anyway, this fellow, George his name was, had been taking me out for three months. Three whole months. It seemed a lifetime to me, quite long enough for me to consider him as a possible husband. But he had his faults and his worst fault was his meanness. Oh, he was a shocker for being mean!

When we went to the pictures he'd buy a quarter pound of chocolates, supposedly for me to eat in the cinema, then he'd hold them in his hand or on his lap, and proceed to gobble them up himself. I soon learned. Directly we sat down our arms used to swing like pendulums and within three minutes the chocolates had gone, the bag thrown under the seat, and we'd settle down to watch the picture.

Another mean streak was the way he passed all the pubs. That was the biggest failing of the lot. Pubs in those days were places you couldn't go into on your own, or even with another girl. If you did, even if you went in with another girl, you got a bad reputation. Everyone felt that you were easy meat, and they treated you that way too. The fact that you'd rather have a drink than a cup of tea was nothing to do with it. It just wasn't done. My mother and father used to like to go out at night and have a drink. They didn't drink much, perhaps they'd have two half-pints of beer or bitter each. It was strong then, and much cheaper because it was stronger. If you had two half-pints you felt the effects; now you can drink enough to blow you out like a balloon and you get home feeling flat as a pancake. If my mother and father wanted to go to the pub they took me with them. You weren't supposed to go in at fourteen, which was when I first started, but then I was always an enormous size and looked well over my age. I drank lemonade at first, then I progressed to shandy, and from there to bitter, and I got used to going in the pub. It wasn't so much for the drink, it was for the life.

Pubs in those days had life. A pub now is only one degree removed from a morgue, isn't it? Nobody speaks to anyone, there's no life or gaiety. Especially now that they're all made into cocktail-lounge type of places. The other day we went into a pub and there was a man humming to himself. He'd had a few drinks, but he was doing no harm, just being happy. Twice the manager came round and told him to stop, and the third time they ejected him. You mustn't enjoy pubs. I used to go into one on a Saturday night with my Mum and Dad before I even went into service. It would be crammed with people, you'd stand there holding your glass right up close to your chest, but you felt happy and it was lively, it was life. That's how I started drinking. I liked the life of the pubs, and I still do. I'd rather go in a pub and have a drink than go anywhere. Luckily, my husband feels the same. (Yes, I got one in the end.) So if we've got any money we whoop it up, if not we just have a couple of beers.

Leaving aside the life you get in a pub, there was another reason that I resented George not taking me there and that's the effect drinks have on you. I used to feel amorous after a couple or so and so did any young man. Any fellow I met who had a face like the back of a bus and who I wouldn't have looked twice at if I'd have been stone-cold sober, looked like Rudolph Valentino after a beer or so. Mind you, I had to be careful not to have too many, there was a borderline, you wanted enough so that they would kiss you and make a fuss of you and so that you could leave them thinking that next time it might be all right to go a bit further, but you didn't want them dashing at you like madmen the very first time they took you home. After all's said and done, you've only got one lot of goods and if you're going to distribute them to all and sundry you haven't got anything worth keeping when the real one comes along! Anyway, every time we got to a pub this George would say to me, 'Would you like a drink?' so I'd say, 'Well, if you would, I would,' then he'd say, 'Well, if you would,' and then I'd say, 'Not unless you would,' and by this time we'd passed the pub and I never did get him inside. I didn't like to look too eager because after all, I was thinking about George as a permanent institution, and I didn't like it to look as if all I thought about was rushing into a pub.

So after a month or two of going out regular; just going to the pictures, the cheapest seats, gobbling a quarter of sweets between us, and never going in a pub, I very reluctantly decided that George would have to have his cards. After all, if a man doesn't spend much on you when you're not married to him, it's a sure thing he's not going to afterwards. If he's not going to take you into a pub when he's already out with you, you can't see him leaving the fireside to go, can you?

When I look back on it now, I just made the efforts to keep him, and put myself out that way because the selection was so poor. When all's said and done, he was a wretched little specimen; he wasn't even as tall as me, and he had no conversation of any kind. He made these model things, model aeroplanes. He told me he had a marvellous collection. Can't you imagine it, a lot of old dust-harbourers they are, you can't do anything with them, and they clutter up the place. I bet somebody's got him now, and cursing him and his flipping aeroplanes. But the interest I used to show in them! I'd say, 'Oh marvellous, can you really make them? I'd love to see a model,' and when he brought one round I stood cooing over it when I couldn't really give twopence for it. The lies you had to tell men to make out that you were interested in them, simply because there was no selection. Girls nowadays if they don't like what a fellow does or what he looks like, they tell him to run after his tail. But not then, no fear you didn't.

Of course, there were some old men about, there always seem to be, and they tell you they're as young as they feel. That's all very well but if they look about ninety it does make a difference, doesn't it? Some of them don't feel all that good either.

I stayed a year with Mrs Bishop. By this time I thought I really ought to get a job where there were more servants and I could have a kitchen maid. So I answered an advertisement in the *Morning Post*; I thought I'd go back to London again.

The house was in Montpelier Square, Knightsbridge. They were Dutch people, bankers, very wealthy, solid, and respectable. He looked just how I envisaged a Dutch banker should look; tremendous corporation, with a gold watch-chain across it.

It was in this house that I saw the change in the status of domestic servants. In other places I'd noticed what must have been the beginnings, but here I found a complete change. Here we really counted as part of the household.

Including the lady's maid, there were seven servants, and we each had a bedroom of our own. And very comfortable rooms they were, and our tastes were consulted. I was asked if there was anything I wanted changed, if I had enough clothes on the bed, if I wanted any more lights in the room, and that kind of thing. It was obvious that they really did want you, and appreciated you being there.

The kitchen was furnished with every appliance that was then known, and although it was still in the basement, it was light and airy, painted white, none of this chocolate brown half up the walls, and green the rest. In the scullery the sink was white enamel, not one of those cement affairs, and aluminium saucepans, which was a change from either iron or copper.

Everything had been bought especially for the staff, none of that 'this will do for the basement'. All our uniforms were provided free. I'd always had to buy all my own uniforms before, the parlourmaid, the housemaid, and the kitchen maid all had striped print dresses, and they were allowed to choose what colour they liked, any shade, pink, or green, or blue. As the cook I was allowed to choose my own colour scheme and style. I had various patterns shown to me. It was all so different.

Madam was very strict. Everything had to be just right, but then she'd paid for it. Meals had to be served absolutely to time, and every dish cooked to perfection. But now I felt she had the right to expect it. She had shown she cared for us. It was up to us to care for them.

Some of the meals she used to plan herself, others I used to work out; sometimes a whole menu, which I'd never been used to doing. I did make some mistakes at first. There were so many things that I'd not done before, or even seen done. But I had old Mother Beeton to rely on. I don't think she ever failed anyone; she'd got recipes for everything under the sun. I know people laugh today about how it says, 'Take twelve eggs and a pint of cream' but of course in those days you did take twelve eggs and a pint of cream.

Having a kitchen maid was quite a help of course, but I wasn't really a lot of good with her because I had such strong recollections of the terrible time when I was in that position and I was determined that I'd never be that harsh when I was a cook. But I found it was quite true what that old harridan of a Mrs Bowchard used to say; that you've got to go around nagging at the kitchen maid.

This one I had there, unless you went for her all the time she didn't bother, and I couldn't be strict enough. I wasn't used to being in a position of authority, I couldn't order her to do something. I'd ask her to and if she was a long time doing it I'd set to and do it myself. Well, that's not the right training for a girl, really and truly. Still there it was, I just couldn't go around nagging at her, saying she was no good, that she'd got to pull her socks up and being generally foul. For one thing it wasn't my nature and for another it seemed just as quick to do it myself. But it wasn't good training for her. I think I failed her.

Madam didn't fail me. At first I found it hard to believe in her interest and concern. I mean after years of poor food, poor surroundings I'd become convinced nothing short of a bloody revolution would get better conditions for domestic workers. Yet after I'd been there a few weeks I realized that Madam really wanted us to be satisfied with our jobs. It's not that she loved the lower classes, she didn't, but she believed that a contented staff made for a well-run household, which it did. Because servants that feel they're being put upon can make it hard in the house in various ways like not rushing to answer the bell, looking sullen, dumb insolence, and petty irritations to make up for what you're not getting. Not there they didn't. As I say Madam didn't love us, we didn't want her to, we wanted what we got; being well paid and doing a good job in return.

I became very proficient as a cook there and I know my efforts were appreciated not only by those upstairs but by the staff, in particular by the butler, Mr Kite.

He was a man about fifty years old, and he'd been in domestic service since he was thirteen; he started as a page-boy and worked his way up. His first place was a country house where the staff included six footmen, two stewards and still-room maids, six housemaids, a chef, an under-chef, four kitchen helpers, and fourteen gardeners; a tremendous establishment! The outside staff lived in cottages on the estate, but the inside staff had the whole top part of the house to themselves. Mind you the men were rigidly segregated from the women, and if one of the men servants was ever found anywhere in the women's section after they had retired for the night, he was instantly dismissed without a reference.

I asked Mr Kite what it was like working in those conditions, and he said, 'Oh, they were real gentry'. 'In what way were they different from our employers here, then?' I asked. Mr Kite said, 'Well, they were so far above the servants that they literally didn't see them. I remember one evening when I'd risen to be a footman, I was waiting at the dinner table after the ladies had retired and the port was being circulated, and the gentlemen were talking about a very scandalous rumour that involved royalty, and they were all adding their quota to the rumour. One of the guests remarked, "We must be careful that nobody overhears us," to which the host replied, "How could they overhear us? We're alone here," and at that time there were three footmen in the room. But we must have been invisible. So that's how much above us they were, literally to them we weren't there.'

One thing I used to envy the people upstairs for was the way they spoke. I used to wish with all my heart that I could speak with their cultured voices. I said to Mr Kite once, 'You know, if only we could speak in the way they do it wouldn't matter if we hadn't got twopence in our pockets, we could walk into the Ritz and as soon as we opened our mouths the waiters would rush to show us to a table; whereas like we are now, if we went in with fifty pounds and asked for a table the only place they would show us to would be the door.'

But Mr Kite was a bit prosy; he sort of mixed with the people above and he got, like so many did, to be like them in lots of ways. He used to bring out platitudes as though they were pearls of wisdom. He really liked being a butler; he used to say, 'I wouldn't change places with any man, there's no shame in honest toil.' I don't know what he meant by *honest* toil, there's a lot of dishonest things being done, but I'm sure toil isn't one of them! Then he'd say, 'There's only two things in life that a man needs; comfort and love.'

Madam supplied all his comfort, I often wondered if I should supply the love. Not that he ever asked me to do so, but I dare say that propinquity and my cooking would have brought him up to scratch if I'd set my heart on having him as a husband. But that would have meant staying in domestic service for ever; a prospect that I couldn't bear to contemplate. Anyway, this was the time I realized my lifelong ambition, I did get married from this place, and it was my last permanent job in service.

# 26

Looking back on my years in domestic service I've often wondered why the status of our work was so low. Why we were all derogatively labelled 'skivvy'. Perhaps it was the intimate nature of our work, I often used to think that was it, the waiting hand and foot on, and almost spoon-feeding people who were quite capable of looking after themselves. In some ways we weren't much better off than serfs, inasmuch as our whole life was regulated by our employers; the hours we worked, the clothes we wore – definitely the clothes we wore at work, and to some extent the clothes we wore when we went out. Even our very scanty free time was overshadowed by the thought that we 'mustn't be in later than ten o'clock'. We weren't free in any way. So maybe that was the reason why the work and those that did it were looked down on, because we were, as it were, bound to our employers.

The employers always claimed that the training they gave you stood you in good stead when you left and married and had a family of your own. When I left domestic service I took with me the knowledge of how to cook an elaborate seven-course dinner and an enormous inferiority complex; I can't say that I found those an asset to my married life.

My husband was a milkman and he earned three pounds five shillings a week, out of which he gave me three pounds, so the ability to cook a seven-course dinner was no help at all. I promptly had to unlearn all the elaborate cooking I had done and fall back on the sort of cooking that my mother did when she brought us up. And all the pleasure I had in cooking disappeared in having to do that sort of cooking.

Mind you, when I first got married I used to do a lot of fancy dishes. I thought that my husband would like it. I used to go to a lot of trouble, with cheaper cuts of meat of course. It involved a lot of work, and when it was over my husband would say, 'Not bad, old girl, but I'd just as soon have fish and chips.' That soon knocked the gilt off the gingerbread to my mind.

Well, every art requires appreciation, doesn't it? I mean people who paint, sculpt, or write books want an audience, that's the reason they're doing it for, and it's the same when you're a cook. You need somebody who savours it, not one who just says, 'Oh, it's not bad.'

Anyway I soon got rid of the seven-course-dinner complex, but the inferiority complex took me far longer to eradicate. I tried. At that time psychiatry and psychology and all that ballyhoo were beginning to be the big thing, and there were no end of books published about how to avoid blushing and what to do about an inferiority complex; so I got one, thinking I might find out what to do about mine. Not only did I read books about it, but I went to classes where I discovered that the complex manifests itself in two forms; either you're timid or you're aggressive. I'd got the latter form. I can assure you it was a far from endearing trait, and it did nothing towards my ambition of 'how to make friends and influence people'! With no money, not good-looking, and very aggressive, you make very few friends and you influence nobody at all. I came to the conclusion that aggression only achieved results when it was allied to beauty or power. Well, I had neither of these desirable traits, so common sense should have taken over from there and convinced me that my position in life was just to be a sort of downtrodden housewife, one of the great army of housewives who've got aspirations, but never manage to do anything about it.

As well as books I had advice from people – it's amazing the amount of people that are always so lavish with their advice, isn't it? It would be, 'What you need is to have a family', or 'You need to educate yourself', or 'What you need is to travel'. Well, as the first of these exhortations was the easiest to accomplish I decided to go in for that. And it certainly occupied my time because I had three children in five years. Three boys. I got quite blasé about it.

I remember when the last one arrived it was a Sunday. Incidentally, all my three children were born on Sundays, I don't know if that means anything or not. My husband went to fetch the midwife, who was just going to church, and was far from pleased about it, though how she thought you could possibly regulate when they were going to come, I don't know. Anyway, the sight of her gloomy face didn't help me at all – having a baby isn't a picnic at the best of times. When it arrived she said, 'Oh what a pity it's another boy.' So I said, 'Well, I don't care if it's a blooming monkey so long as it's got here at last!' She looked at me in shocked amazement and said, 'You know, I look upon every child I deliver as a flower sent down from above to be planted in the earth's soil.' This kind of talk from someone who had produced no flowers at all – she was a spinster – made me say, 'What about all the seed that falls on stony ground?'

I took a very prosaic view of the whole proceeding, because when I was a child I'd lived in a street where most babies were born as a result of Saturday night revels. They were all known as 'beer babies'.

When Albert and I decided to get married naturally I wanted to leave service straight away. After all's said and done, all my working years had been building up to the fact that by getting married I could get away from it with all possible speed and rapidity. So when the date was set I gave a month's notice.

This time I had a perfectly legitimate reason for doing so and Madam was very pleasant about it. It was a funny thing that although none of them really liked you to leave if you were going to another job, if you left to get married it was a totally different thing. It was acceptable and it was re-spectable.

And yet the business of getting a young man was not respectable, and one's employers tended to degrade any relationship. It seemed to me one was expected to find husbands under a gooseberry bush. Their daughters were debs, and they could meet young men at balls, dances, and private parties, but if any of the servants had boyfriends they were known as 'followers'. I think 'followers' is a degrading term, it brings to your mind people slinking through back streets, not seeing the light of day, with any young man that cares for you. Why should you have to do that? Why should the fact that you're a servant and in love be wrong when the whole deb set-up was manufactured to bring their daughters together with young men? They could have said, 'If you have a young man you're interested in, you can ask him in to the servants' hall when you've finished your work.' But no, you had to slink up the area steps and meet him on the corner of the road on some pretext like going to post a letter. And on your night out when you came back you couldn't stand at the top of the area steps with him or bring him down to say goodnight to him. He wasn't a young man, he was a 'follower'. They made you feel that there was something intrinsically bad in having a member of the opposite sex interested in you at all.

We decided to get married in a registry office. We hadn't got much money, and Albert and I didn't think much of all the pomp and ceremony. It was a quiet affair. I got all the usual inquisitive remarks. Such things as, 'You're getting married to get out of service', and, 'Are you really in love?' I wasn't madly in love, but I cared about him, which I thought was a good basis to get married on.

In view of the fact that my husband only earned three

pounds five a week, of which I had three, you might wonder why I didn't go out to work. Women simply didn't then. Working-class husbands bitterly resented the very thought that their wives should have to work outside the home. It seemed to cast a slur on the husband and implied that he wasn't capable of keeping you. If a man was unemployed, well that was a different thing. Then you had to.

Our first home was in Chelsea and there was a woman living in the basement next door to us who was married to a Russian, a Mrs Balkonsky, her name was; her husband was of course Boris. She had five children, and she got about the same money as I did. She was an extremely good milliner, an occupation that she could have followed in her own home, and supplemented the family income. Yet her husband was so against her doing any work or making any money apart from what he gave her, that she wasn't allowed to.

Mind you, I didn't want to go out to work. The time never hung on my hands at all, I was only too glad to have nothing to do for a while. Although I was a feminist and stuck up for the rights of women, it didn't go that far. I asserted an independence as regards the running of the home, I wasn't subservient in any way to my husband. I considered that he received good value for the money he gave me in every way; in the physical relationship, in the running of the home, in the social relationships too, and I considered that I wasn't under any obligation to him at all.

In any case the only kind of work that I knew how to do well was cooking and to do that would have meant going out at night and doing dinners. Well, I don't think that the wife going to work at night is a very good basis for a marriage relationship.

I wanted to make a success of marriage as I wanted to make a success of other things in life. And so much of my time had been spent thinking about getting out of service that it was a long while before I felt that home life wasn't enough, and by then I had collected a family of three children, so that any aspirations I had had to go by the board for the time being. Looking after three children is a fulltime job to me at any rate, because I was a mother in the full sense of the word, I think.

As I've said, after we got married we lived in what we considered was the best part of London, Chelsea. We paid fifteen shillings a week for a bed-sitting-room, with a minute little kitchen. We had the first child there. But naturally as the family increased, one room and kitchen wasn't enough so we had to move. We went in turn to Willesden, Harlesden, and Kilburn. They're very dreary, dingy places with houses to match the kind of locality.

I had three children in the first five years of my marriage and by then – Albert was still a milkman – money was getting a bit tight.

When our eldest child was about five years old I happened to be out one day and I met one of the maids who I'd been in service with. She told me that the people she was working for were at their wits' end because the cook was away and they'd got to give a dinner party. She said, 'Why don't you come in and cook the dinner for them?' I said, 'I couldn't, I haven't done that sort of cooking for years.' 'You'll pick it up again straight away, you can't forget that kind of thing. Why don't you try?' So I went home and spoke to Albert about it. I put it to him. It would mean at least ten shillings or a guinea for doing it, and the money would be very handy for the children. So he agreed and I did it.

I made quite a good job of it too, and after it was over the lady of the house came down and asked me if I would like her to recommend me to her friends. I said 'Yes'. From time to time people that she knew would write to me and ask me if I could come and do a dinner; sometimes for six, sometimes as many as twelve, in which case they would have some dishes in from outside as well. When it was a small dinner I got half a guinea, but for an elaborate one I earned two guineas, and when you consider that my husband was only getting about four pounds a week even then, two guineas was a lot of money indeed. And I quite enjoyed these little expeditions. Apart from the money it gave me an insight into a different kind of life. People were so different, so friendly. They'd be in and out of the kitchen talking to you as though you were one of them. In domestic work things had certainly changed.

# 27

THIS WAY of life passed pleasantly enough until 1942 when my husband was called up. Albert was conscripted into the Royal Air Force, so I decided that I'd move back down to Hove.

I didn't want to stay in London in wartime with three young boys, so I wrote to my parents to see if they could get me a house. It was quite easy to get houses in Hove at that time because a lot of people had left. They didn't like the hit-and-run raids they were having there. They got me a six-roomed house for a pound a week. It was marvellous, the first house we'd had since we'd been married. The most we'd ever lived in before was three rooms and a share of lavatory.

I remember one place we had at Kilburn, we had to go downstairs and walk through someone's kitchen to get to the lavatory. All through the summer the man used to sit right outside the lavatory door on a deckchair, and it was most embarrassing to ask him to move. I'm sure that's where I first suffered with constipation!

Now everything would be my own, I thought. I was in

clover. You can imagine what our stuff looked like in it, because we only had enough for three rooms. It had to be spread all around. I just had one bed in each bedroom, nothing on the floor, but I didn't care.

All the boys got on well in Hove; they all went to the same elementary school at first, and then they passed the examinations to get to the grammar school. While this was a great joy, it was also a terrible worry. With three young boys to look after on my own I couldn't go out to work, and the separation allowance that I got at that time was very poor indeed.

It wasn't until I'd written goodness knows how many letters to the Education Authorities that I managed to get more money. But I found great difficulty in managing even so, and each time Albert got a promotion – he was eventually made up to corporal – we didn't benefit, because out of his increased money the government docked my allowance. So there was no incentive for him to try to get further.

I couldn't make the boys' clothes now. If they'd been girls I could have, but boys have got to look the same as everybody else. You can't send them to school in home-made suits.

I remember one terrible occasion, the only time in my life when I had to apply for charity. They only had one pair of shoes each and although when my husband was home he used to mend them, he had been posted overseas. I was at my wits' end as to how to get them repaired. So I went down to the Soldiers', Sailors', and Airmen's Association who sent me over to the Council. It was something too terrible for words. You need a hide like a rhinoceros, it seemed to me, to ask them for anything. Some people were used to getting all and sundry. They never turned a hair. But this was the first time I had ever asked for anything. I went in very nervous with a face as red as a beetroot. I felt like a pauper. 'Why do you want shoes for them? Why haven't they got shoes?' I said, 'They've only got one pair.' 'Why don't you get them mended?' they asked. 'I can get them mended,' I said, 'but in the meantime they won't be able to go to school. They've got no others.' After this kind of talk they returned me to the Soldiers', Sailors', and Airmen's place. I went back to them and I said, 'They said it comes under your jurisdiction,' and they said, 'It doesn't, not to supply shoes. You go back to the Council and start again.' When I went back and through the whole process again, they grudgingly gave me some forms. They don't give you money and they don't give you shoes, they give you forms to take to a special shop in Hove.

They wouldn't let you have shoes, you had to have boots, charity boots. My sons had never worn boots before. I never entered fully into how much they must have felt it. I was so obsessed with how I felt, I never investigated their feelings. Going to school wearing boots, and everyone knowing that they're charity boots because they were a special kind.

When my boys went to this grammar school, it was still a fee-paying school. So naturally the parents of the boys that were there were far better off financially than we were. A lot of them had been to preparatory schools. And they had money. Some of the boys had a pound a week for pocket money. A pound a week! I couldn't give mine a shilling. I remember when I had a bit of trouble with one of them – he drew a moustache on the headmaster's photo – the headmaster saying to me that it was all poppycock their feeling inferior because they hadn't got money. 'I came up the hard way,' he said, 'I only got to a grammar school on scholarship level, and I only had sixpence a week pocket money.' But times had altered. People had more money then.

Another terrible thing was that if you had an income of under five pounds a week you were entitled to free dinners. Well, there was no one else in any of their classes that had free dinners, and each new term the master would say, 'Stand up those who want tickets for dinners.' Well, you just imagine how you would feel if you're the only child in the class whose parents can't afford to pay for your dinners. I didn't fully understand it myself at the time. If I had realized the situation I wouldn't have been ambitious to get them to a grammar school, I really wouldn't. I used to write to the master in advance, I knew which one they would have, and say, 'Will you please not say out loud, "Who is going to have a free school dinner?".' I admit they did take notice then, and they didn't do it.

Another thing that I didn't realize was sport. Cricket for instance. I couldn't buy cricket flannels or cricket boots. I ran up football shorts for them, but I couldn't afford the journeys for away matches. I thought, it doesn't matter, they're getting a good education, that's what matters. But those other things did matter.

I think that one can be too ambitious. You educate them, you send them into a social community of which they can't be one. People have the same herd instinct as animals. There's only got to be one that's different and they kick hell out of him.

# 28

WITH THIS struggle on I decided to go out to work. I decided to do housework again. I couldn't take on cooking because there wasn't a lot of work for cooks in wartime. It had to be housework. It was very poorly paid at that time. When I first started I got tenpence an hour. It seems fantastic now when you think about it. I suppose everyone must have been getting the same otherwise I'm sure I would have asked for more.

I worked for a vicar, which was jolly hard work. You know what vicarages are; there's the day for the boy scouts, the day for the girl guides, the day for the Women's Institute, the Mothers' Union, and of course these old vicarages are not labour-saving places. They were planned with a house full of servants in mind. Still I enjoyed it there. The money was bad, but there were perks; left-over food, and when there was a jumble sale the vicar's wife always used to let me pick out anything I wanted first. She'd say, 'Just give a few coppers and take your choice,' and many a decent suit or jersey I got for the boys before the horde came in.

I stayed at the vicarage job for some time, and then one day I was chatting to a friend who was also doing domestic work and she told me she was getting is 1s 3d an hour; the rate had gone up fivepence an hour in a comparatively short time. Well, there's only one reason for doing that kind of work, money, so I started to look round for another job.

The first thing that amazed me was the difference that I found after so many years. Large houses that were once opulently furnished and had had a large staff were now reduced to no staff at all; just someone coming in for a few hours daily. Much of their lovely stuff had gone; they had had to sell it to pay their income tax.

Most of these ladies were very elderly and they accepted this change in their status with fortitude. Some of them used to talk to me about their changed circumstances and their vanished possessions. I remember one house where I worked, I used to go there two mornings a week. All they had left of their silver was a large tray, one of those which a whole tea set is carried on, and one day when I was polishing this, Mrs Jackson, a very elderly lady, said to me, 'Ah, Margaret, when the silver service stood on that tray, and when the butler carried it into the drawing-room, it used to look a picture of safety and security,' she said. 'We never thought that our way of life would change.'

I couldn't help feeling sorry for them, even though judged by my income they were still fairly well off. It's much harder to be poor, isn't it, when for years you've had money rolling in, than if you've never had money at all; and then to come down to doing such a lot of their own work at their age. It's easy to turn to when you're young, you're resilient.

Mind you, the funny part was that even though now they could only afford dailies, some of them still retained their old autocratic ways. They used bitterly to complain about the sordidness of life, they were very fond of saying that, that everything was 'sordid'. And their favourite was, 'The working class are aping their betters', the betters being them of course, and 'The country is being run by a collection of nobodies and is going down the drain'.

One of the ladies I worked for was a Mrs Rutherford-Smith. One day she said to me, 'Margaret, you're a very good worker, and I like you, but you've got one failing and I hope you won't be offended when I tell you what that failing is. You never call me "Madam".' And then she added, 'You know, Margaret, if I was talking to the Queen I should say "Madam" to her.' I wanted to reply, 'Well, there's only one Queen but there's thousands of Mrs Smiths!'

Mrs Rutherford-Smith and those like her missed all those little attentions that used to be their prerogative, the hat-raising, the deference from tradesmen, and the being waited on by well-trained servants.

Many of the people for whom I was a daily were old and lonely, and I was the only person who provided them with contact with life outside. This seemed strange because many of them lived in flats, and you'd think that living in a block of flats you'd be in a sort of microcosm of life. But it just isn't so. I've worked in half a dozen such blocks and I've never met a person either going in or coming out. Everyone seemed to be isolated in their own little cell. They needed to live in them as they were easy to run. But it was a very lonely life for them.

Some who had adopted a philosophical view talked to you as though you were one of themselves, but others felt that they were really doing a great kindness in sitting down with you and being on equal terms with you. They thought it was very odd that a daily should show any signs of intelligence.

There was a Mrs Swob that I worked for. I shouldn't really call her name 'Swob' – it was spelt Schwab, and she pronounced it 'Swayb'; that's how she liked it pronounced, but much to her fury most people pronounced it Swob.

This Mrs Schwab's house was filled with antiques, terrible old dust-collectors, especially some round mirrors that she had, with convoluted gilt frames, and she showed no signs of pleasure when I knocked one of the knobs off one of these frames. 'You must treat things better, Margaret,' she said. 'Don't you love good objects?' 'No, I don't, Mrs Schwab,' I said. 'To me they're just material things; I have an affinity with G. K. Chesterton who wrote about the malignity of inanimate objects,' I said, 'and I think they are malign because they take up so much of my time, dusting, polishing, and cleaning them. Look at that vase,' I said, 'that you say is worth a hundred pounds, if that was to drop on the floor and break it would just be three or four worthless bits of china.' That set her back on her heels for a few seconds. 'I didn't know you read, Margaret,' she said. 'I read a lot of course.' She was one of those, whatever you did, she did it, only ten times more.

I was talking about films once. 'Oh yes, I could have been a film star,' she said, 'I wanted to be but at that time I was going out with the man who is now my husband. He wouldn't let me. Everyone was most disappointed.' You'd be amazed all the rubbish I had to listen to, they ladled it all out, and you had to look suitably impressed. You're working for them and you want your money, and if it wasn't them it would be somebody else. They employ you to be a captive audience. Still, while you're listening you're not working.

This Mrs Schwab had one of the most infuriating habits; every time I went she used to say to me, 'When you scrub the bathroom, Margaret, don't forget the corners.' This gained her less than nothing. From then on I never used the scrubbing-brush, I just threw the soap round the floor.

The last straw there was when I was sweeping the balcony. One morning she said to me, 'Oh' don't sweep the dust that way, sweep it the other way.' Well, did you ever hear such drivel? I collected my wages. I hadn't got the nerve to tell her I wasn't coming any more because instinctively I felt she would let loose a flood of invective, she looked that type to me. I wrote a very posh letter, I thought it was, anyway, to the effect that 'it must be as irritating to her to feel that she had to keep telling me how to do things, as it was galling for me to have to listen to her'.

You didn't have to worry about references on a daily job. You just said you'd never been out before, or that the people you last worked for had died. As a matter of fact the last people I worked for had all died. I don't know whether there is any sinister connexion, but they have.

I can't help thinking that people who were once wealthy and now have to live on a fixed income are worse off than ordinary working-class people, working-class people's incomes do rise to meet the cost of living. They can ask for a rise, and go on strike if they don't get it, or they get a cost-of-living bonus. But people who are living on fixed incomes like these old ladies have got to keep on trying to keep up some sort of show. A place like Hove is full of these decayed gentlewomen who are struggling to make ends meet. And in spite of the kind of idiosyncrasies I've mentioned, they do a marvellous job, because they're trying to cope with a way of life that their upbringing gave them no preparation for at all. I've been amazed at the resilience and zest for life of some of these old ladies.

# 29

IT WAS when my youngest son was going to grammar school and my eldest was preparing for the university that I realized we had nothing in common to talk about except the weather. They would come home and discuss history, astronomy, French, and all those kind of things, some of which meant nothing to me. I'd never tried to keep up with the Joneses, but I determined to have a shot at keeping up with the boys.

First of all I thought about taking a correspondence course. But apart from the expense, you're on your own doing a correspondence course; if you don't feel like working there's no one to urge you on, you're not in rivalry with anyone and it doesn't matter how long you take.

Then one of my boys' history masters told me about a course of lectures given by Professor Bruce, Extra-Mural Professor from Oxford. They weren't expensive, I think it was only a shilling a time, or cheaper if you took the whole lot, twenty-four of them. I took the lot.

It was fascinating to me this course of lectures. He must

have been a brilliant teacher because the lessons were in the evening from half past seven to half past nine, with a break in between for a cup of coffee, but often with the discussion that used to go on afterwards it was eleven o'clock before I got away, and eleven thirty before I got home. My husband used to say, 'I don't know what kind of education you're getting that keeps you out till half past eleven.'

But it was a real eye-opener for me, I'd always thought history was a dry thing, a succession of dates and things like that.

Then I started going to evening classes in philosophy, history, and literature. The only thing that really beat me was this metaphysical philosophy. You know when you first start anything, you want to be all high-hat. You don't want to go to the same things that everyone else goes to, you want to come out with some high-falutin' name, so I signed on for metaphysical philosophy.

I never knew what it was all about. All I could understand was it was something to do with being a hedonist, or some such thing. After six evenings I decided that it wasn't for me. But that was the only subject where I didn't stick the course out.

Where has it all taken me? Well, I passed my 'O' levels at the age of fifty-eight, and I'm now taking the Advance levels which I hope to get before I'm sixty. People say to me, 'I can't understand you doing it.'

I think it springs from the beginnings. All life is bound up together, isn't it? I liked school, I won a scholarship which I couldn't afford to take; I went into domestic service. I was dissatisfied and all this dissatisfaction was worked out in my attitudes to the environments of domestic service. If I'd been something else I should have been militant against that life, I expect.

When I got married, I had the boys and became a mother pure and simple. Then when they were off my hands it came out again.

People say, 'I suppose you got bored with life', but it wasn't as sudden as that. The seeds are in you and although it may take ten, twenty, or forty years, eventually you can do what you wanted to do at the beginning.

Would I have been happier if I'd been able to do what I wanted when I was young? I might have been. I'm not one of those who pretend that because you're poor there's something wonderful about it. I'd love to be rich. There's nothing particularly beautiful about being poor, having the wrong sort of clothes, and not being able to go to the right sort of places. I don't particularly envy rich people but I don't blame them. They try and hang on to their money, and if I had it I'd hang on to it too. Those people who say the rich should share what they've got are talking a lot of my eye and Betty Martin; it's only because they haven't got it they think that way. I wouldn't reckon to share mine around.

Looking back on what I've said it may seem as if I was very embittered with my life in domestic service. Bitterness does come to the fore because it was the strong feeling I had; and the experiences are the ones that stay in my mind now.

I know it's all dead and gone. Things like that don't happen now. But I think it's worth not forgetting that they did happen.

But we did have happy times and I did enjoy life. Remember, I'd never been used to a lot of freedom.

Domestic service does give an insight and perhaps an inspiration for a better kind of life. You do think about the way they lived and maybe unbeknown to yourself you try to emulate it. The social graces may not mean very much but they do help you to ease your way through life.

So despite what it may sound like, I'm not embittered about having had to go into domestic service. I do often wonder what would have happened if I could have realized my ambition and been a teacher, but I'm happy now, and as my knowledge increases and my reading widens, I look forward to a happy future.

extracts reading groups
books competitions books new
discounts extracts extracts
competitions reading groups extracts
books new events discounts
events books reading groups
new extracts extracts discounts
books new titles reading groups
interviews events new
reading groups books events extracts books
events extracts interviews new books
discounts new books events
reading groups events new books extracts
events new interviews new
discounts extracts discounts

**www.panmacmillan.com**

extracts events reading groups books
competitions books extracts new